IXL MATH WORKBOOK

GRADE 5
FRACTIONS

ISBN: 9781947569478
24 23 22 21 20 1 2 3 4 5

Printed in the USA

2 Parts of a whole

Write the fraction shown.

$\frac{1}{4}$ ______

______

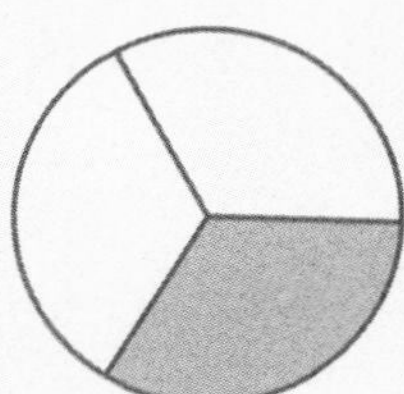

______

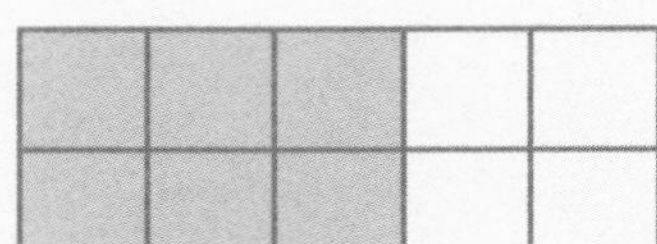

______

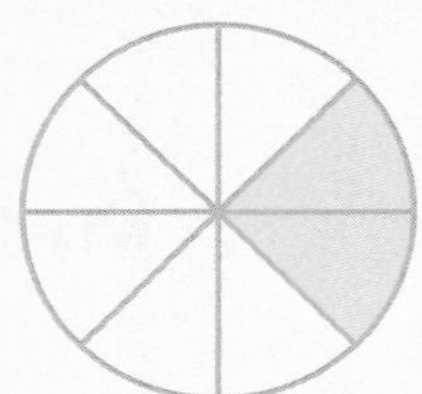

______

______

Shade in each fraction.

$\frac{1}{2}$

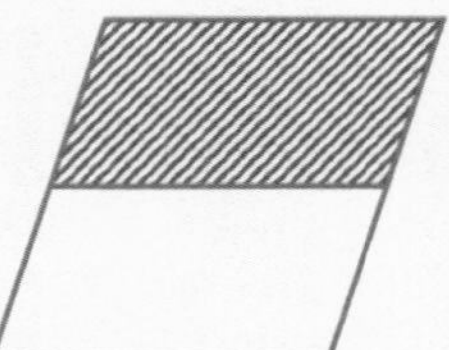

$\frac{3}{4}$

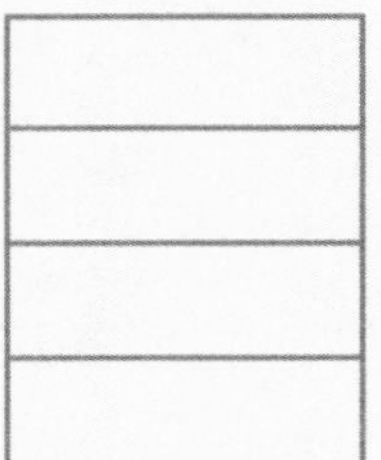

$\frac{7}{8}$

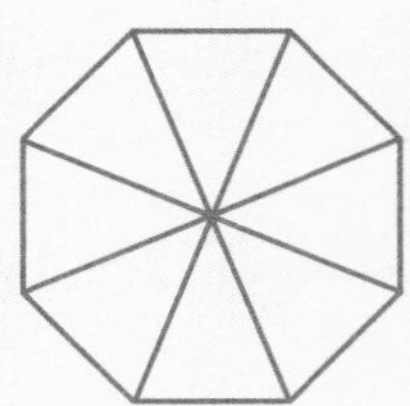

IXL.com
skill ID
PCF

For more practice, visit IXL.com or the IXL mobile app and enter this code in the search bar.

Answer each question.

What fraction of the bicycles have baskets?

$\frac{5}{6}$

What fraction of the envelopes are open?

______

What fraction of the ice cream cones are chocolate?

______

What fraction of the glasses have straws?

______

Shade in each fraction.

$\frac{2}{5}$

$\frac{7}{10}$

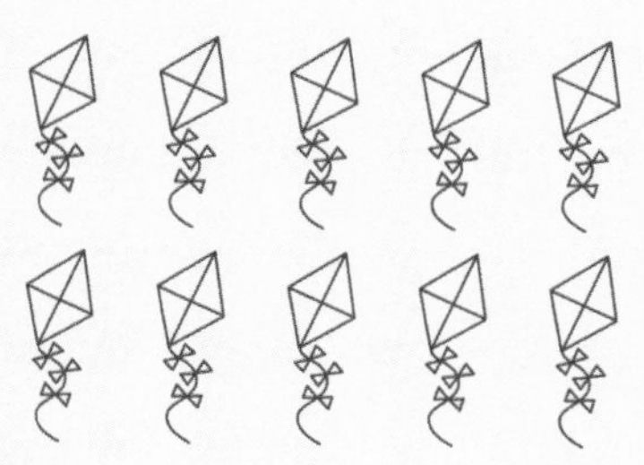

$\frac{3}{6}$

4 Number lines

Write the fraction shown.

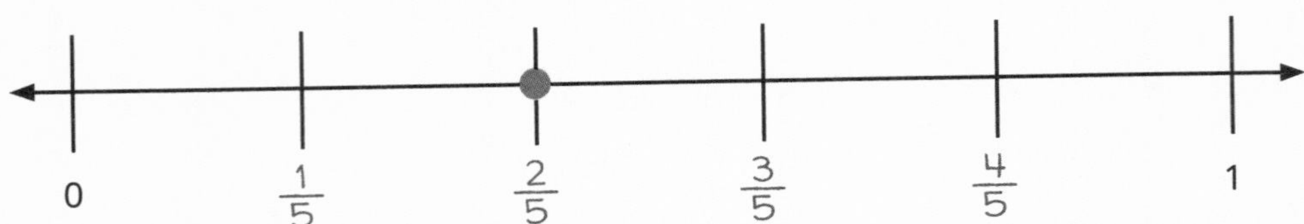

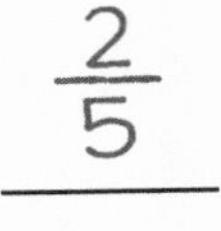

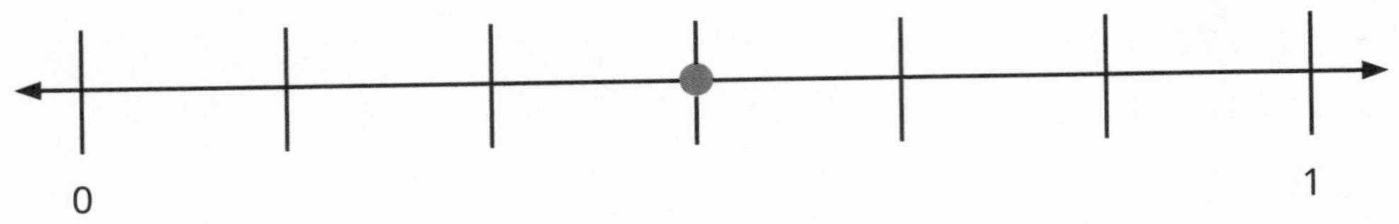

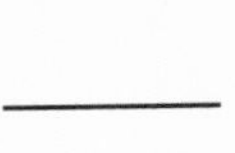

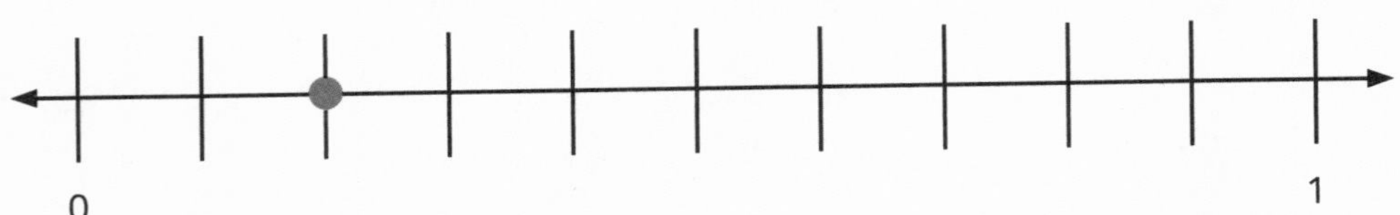

Show each fraction on the number line.

$\frac{1}{4}$

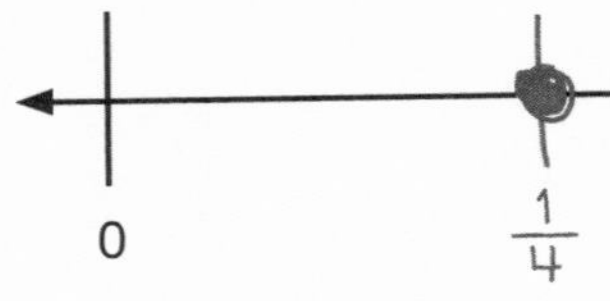

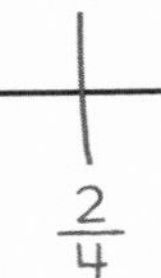

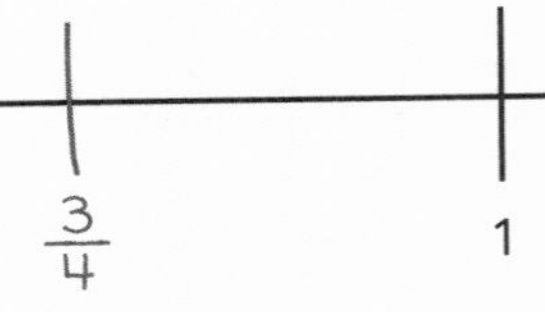

0 1

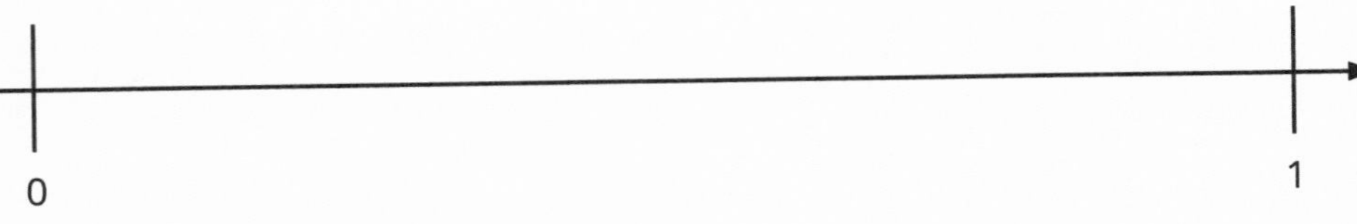

To make an equivalent fraction, multiply or divide the numerator and denominator by the same number. Try it yourself! Write an equivalent fraction for each of the following fractions.

$$\frac{3}{4} \overset{\times 3}{=} \frac{9}{12}$$

$$\frac{4}{6} \overset{\div 2}{=} \frac{2}{3}$$

$\frac{5}{9} =$ ____ $\frac{6}{9} =$ ____

$\frac{1}{10} =$ ____ $\frac{2}{11} =$ ____

$\frac{9}{18} =$ ____ $\frac{10}{24} =$ ____

$\frac{15}{25} =$ ____ $\frac{7}{21} =$ ____

KEEP IT GOING! Can you come up with another equivalent fraction for each problem on this page?

Equivalent fractions

Find the path from start to finish! Move in the direction of each equivalent fraction. Continue until you reach the end.

START ↓

$\frac{1}{4}$	$\frac{4}{16}$	$\frac{12}{15}$	$\frac{3}{5}$	$\frac{2}{20}$
$\frac{1}{8}$		$\frac{4}{5}$		$\frac{1}{10}$
$\frac{2}{3}$	$\frac{7}{14}$	$\frac{1}{2}$	$\frac{6}{14}$	$\frac{3}{5}$
$\frac{4}{6}$		$\frac{3}{9}$		$\frac{9}{10}$
$\frac{8}{9}$	$\frac{16}{18}$	$\frac{7}{12}$	$\frac{14}{24}$	$\frac{2}{8}$
$\frac{24}{30}$		$\frac{14}{20}$		$\frac{4}{16}$
$\frac{1}{3}$	$\frac{7}{9}$	$\frac{14}{18}$	$\frac{1}{3}$	$\frac{9}{27}$
$\frac{8}{24}$		$\frac{1}{4}$		$\frac{1}{4}$
$\frac{6}{21}$	$\frac{2}{7}$	FINISH	$\frac{4}{11}$	$\frac{6}{7}$

Simplest form

Let's Learn!

You can write a fraction in **simplest form** by dividing the numerator and denominator by their **greatest common factor (GCF)**.

Let's try it for $\frac{6}{18}$. To find the GCF, write out the factors of each number. Look at the factors they share, and circle the largest one. The GCF of 6 and 18 is 6.

Factors of 6: 1, 2, 3, (6)

Factors of 18: 1, 2, 3, (6), 9, 18

To get the simplest form of $\frac{6}{18}$, you can divide the top and bottom by the GCF, 6.

$$\frac{6}{18} \xrightarrow{\div 6} = \frac{1}{3}$$

Find the GCF. Then divide to write each fraction in simplest form.

Factors of 7: __________________

Factors of 14: __________________

$\frac{7}{14} = $ ____

Factors of 10: __________________

Factors of 25: __________________

$\frac{10}{25} = $ ____

Factors of 8: __________________

Factors of 22: __________________

$\frac{8}{22} = $ ____

Simplest form

Write each fraction in simplest form.

$\frac{15}{20}$ = ____

$\frac{6}{10}$ = ____

$\frac{3}{24}$ = ____

$\frac{14}{20}$ = ____

$\frac{5}{25}$ = ____

$\frac{9}{18}$ = ____

$\frac{16}{40}$ = ____

$\frac{20}{48}$ = ____

$\frac{5}{45}$ = ____

$\frac{16}{24}$ = ____

$\frac{32}{36}$ = ____

$\frac{18}{30}$ = ____

$\frac{25}{45}$ = ____

$\frac{30}{36}$ = ____

Draw a ◯ around fractions whose simplest form is $\frac{1}{2}$.

Draw a □ around fractions whose simplest form is $\frac{2}{3}$.

Draw a △ around fractions whose simplest form is $\frac{3}{4}$.

Cross out any fractions that have a different simplest form.

$\frac{8}{16}$	$\frac{22}{33}$	$\frac{3}{15}$	$\frac{18}{27}$
$\frac{6}{8}$	$\frac{12}{15}$	$\frac{27}{36}$	$\frac{9}{12}$
$\frac{4}{14}$	$\frac{14}{21}$	$\frac{3}{6}$	$\frac{3}{36}$
$\frac{18}{24}$	$\frac{10}{20}$	$\frac{10}{30}$	$\frac{6}{9}$

IXL.com skill ID **A76**

Adding fractions

Let's Learn!

You can add fractions with like denominators using models.
Try it for $\frac{2}{4} + \frac{1}{4}$.

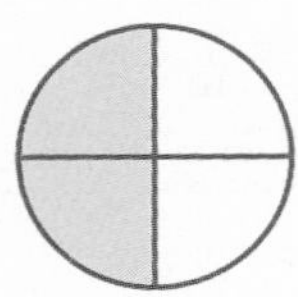
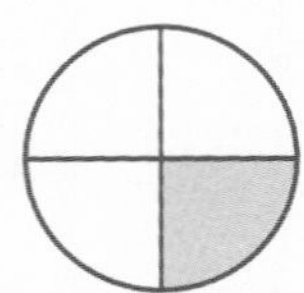
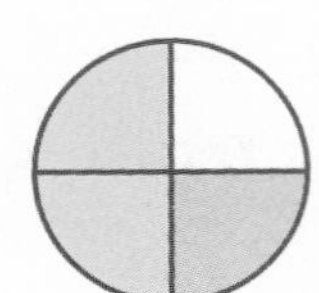

$$\frac{2}{4} + \frac{1}{4} = \frac{3}{4}$$

Add. Shade in the missing fraction.

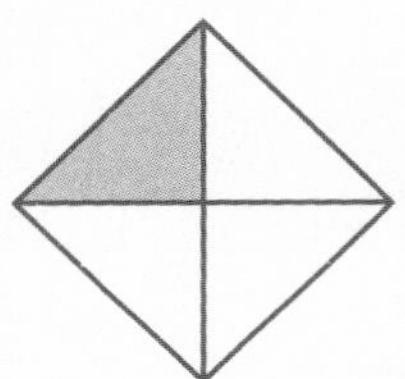
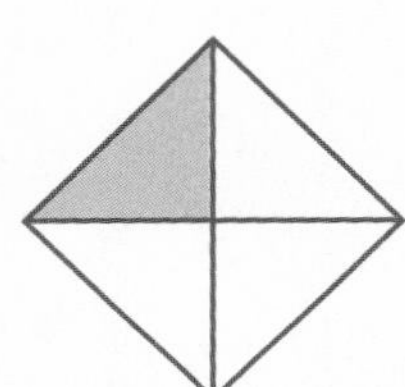
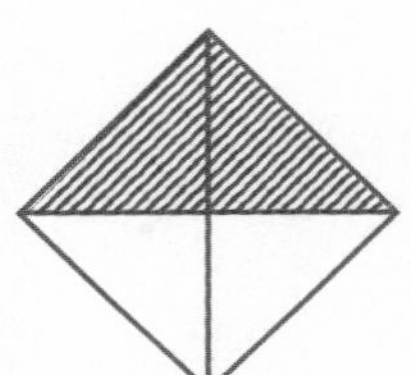

$$\frac{1}{4} + \frac{1}{4} = \frac{2}{4}$$

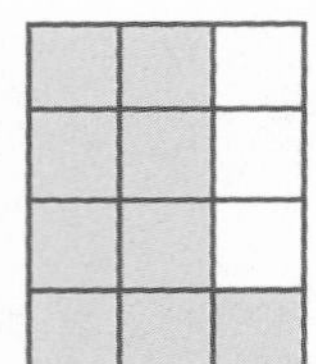
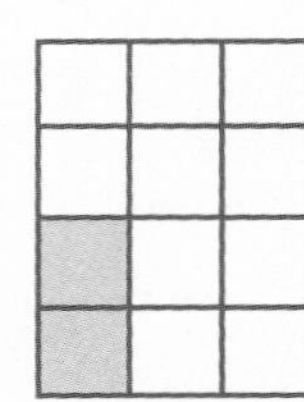
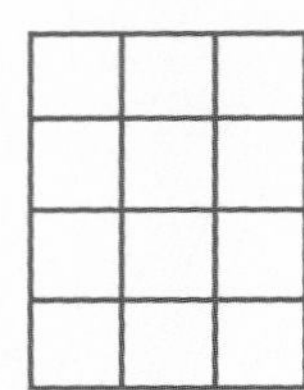

$$\frac{9}{12} + \frac{2}{12} = \_\_\_$$

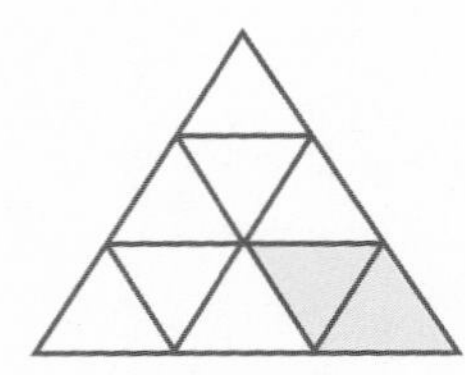
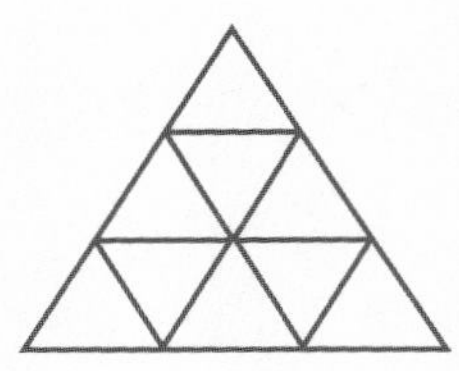

$$\frac{5}{9} + \frac{2}{9} = \_\_\_$$

Let's Learn!

You can also subtract fractions with like denominators. For example, look at $\frac{3}{5}$ - $\frac{1}{5}$.

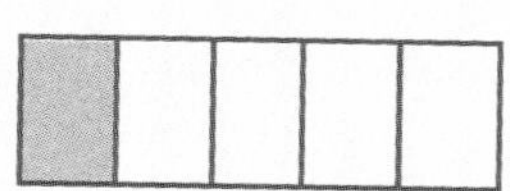
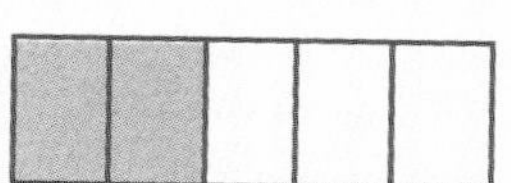

$\frac{3}{5} - \frac{1}{5} = \frac{2}{5}$

Subtract. Shade in the missing fraction.

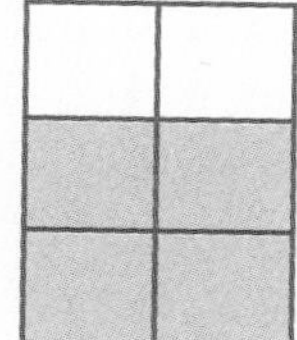
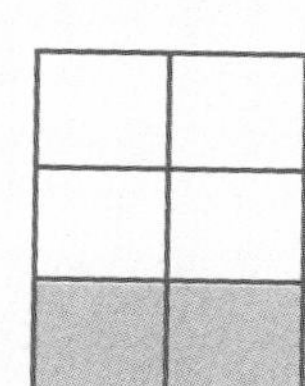
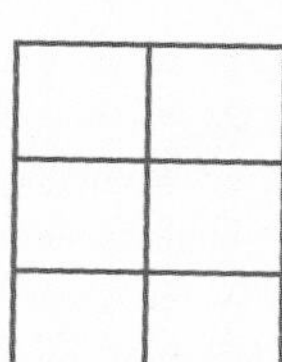

$\frac{4}{6} - \frac{2}{6} =$ ____

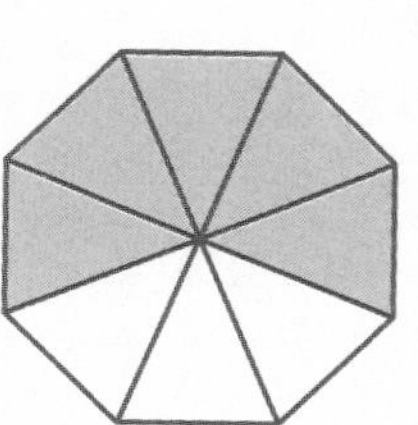
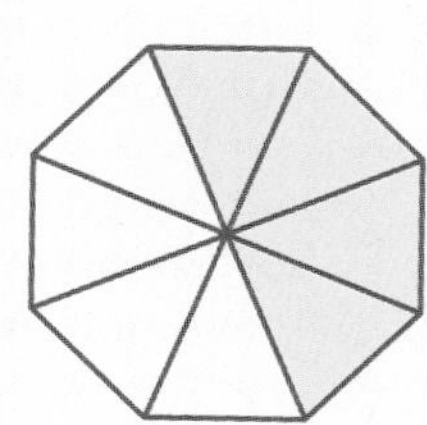
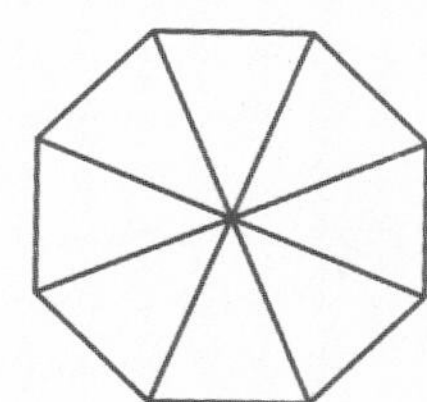

$\frac{5}{8} - \frac{4}{8} =$ ____

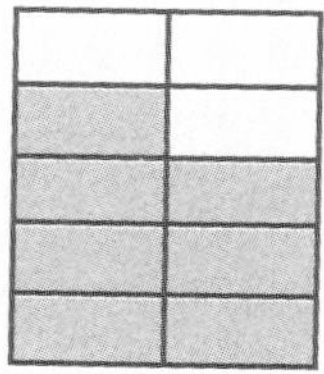
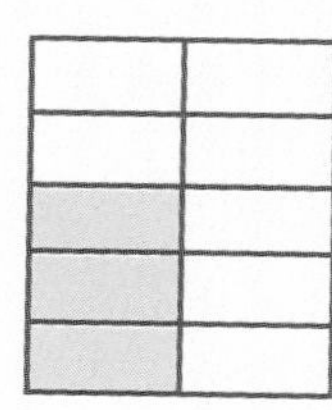
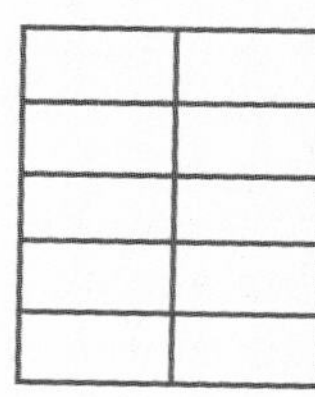

$\frac{7}{10} - \frac{3}{10} =$ ____

12 Adding and subtracting fractions

Let's Learn!

To add or subtract fractions with like denominators, just add or subtract the numerators. The denominators will stay the same!

$\frac{1}{3} + \frac{1}{3} = \frac{2}{3}$ $\frac{5}{7} - \frac{2}{7} = \frac{3}{7}$

Add or subtract. Write your answer in simplest form.

$\frac{2}{9} + \frac{4}{9} =$ $\frac{6}{9} = \frac{2}{3}$

$\frac{9}{10} - \frac{7}{10} =$ ______

$\frac{4}{7} - \frac{1}{7} =$ ______

$\frac{1}{8} + \frac{3}{8} =$ ______

$\frac{4}{15} + \frac{8}{15} =$ ______

$\frac{10}{11} - \frac{2}{11} =$ ______

$\frac{5}{14} + \frac{3}{14} =$ ______

$\frac{7}{12} - \frac{5}{12} =$ ______

Challenge yourself! Add or subtract. Write your answer in simplest form.

$\frac{1}{33} + \frac{4}{33} =$ ______

$\frac{27}{50} - \frac{3}{50} =$ ______

$\frac{7}{29} - \frac{5}{29} =$ ______

$\frac{7}{81} + \frac{2}{81} =$ ______

Fill in the missing numbers.

$\frac{4}{5} - \frac{1}{5} = \frac{3}{5}$

$\frac{3}{13} + \frac{\square}{13} = \frac{12}{13}$

$\frac{\square}{15} + \frac{6}{15} = \frac{13}{15}$

$\frac{9}{10} - \frac{\square}{10} = \frac{1}{10}$

$\frac{1}{6} + \frac{\square}{6} = \frac{5}{6}$

$\frac{10}{11} - \frac{\square}{11} = \frac{6}{11}$

$\frac{\square}{12} - \frac{4}{12} = \frac{3}{12}$

$\frac{\square}{7} + \frac{5}{7} = \frac{6}{7}$

$\frac{2}{18} + \frac{\square}{18} = \frac{16}{18}$

$\frac{11}{17} - \frac{\square}{17} = \frac{5}{17}$

$\frac{\square}{14} - \frac{9}{14} = \frac{3}{14}$

$\frac{7}{20} + \frac{\square}{20} = \frac{15}{20}$

$\frac{\square}{19} + \frac{4}{19} = \frac{17}{19}$

Adding fractions

Let's Learn!

To add fractions with different denominators, make equivalent fractions with the same denominator. Then add! Try it for $\frac{1}{2} + \frac{1}{7}$.

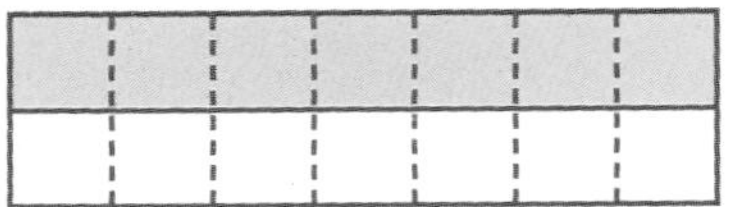
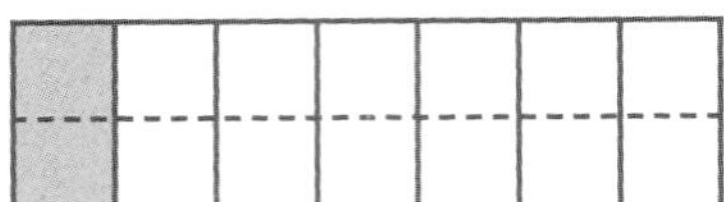
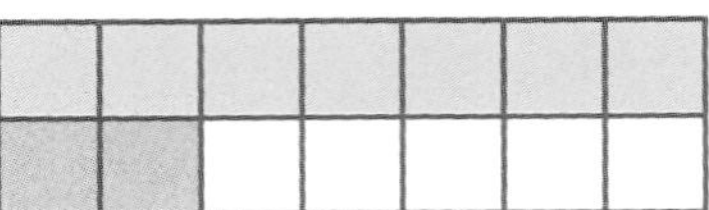

$\frac{7}{14}$ ~~$\frac{1}{2}$~~ $+$ $\frac{2}{14}$ ~~$\frac{1}{7}$~~ $= \frac{9}{14}$

Add. Shade in the missing fraction.

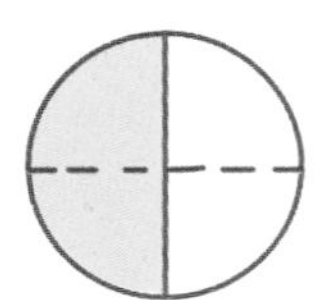
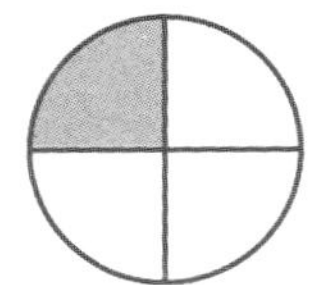
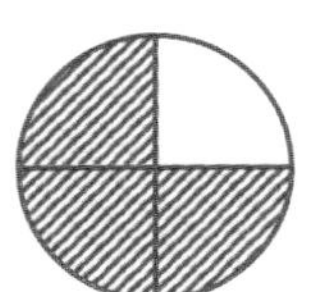

$\frac{2}{4}$ ~~$\frac{1}{2}$~~ $+ \frac{1}{4} = \frac{3}{4}$

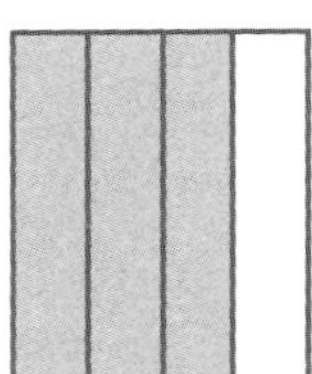
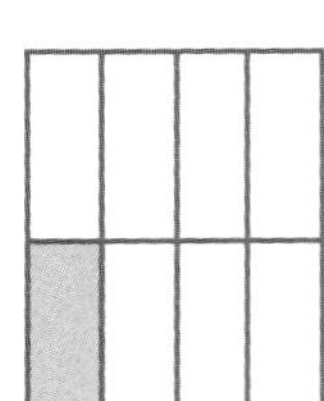
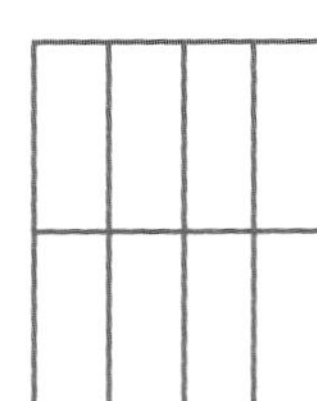

$\frac{3}{4} + \frac{1}{8} =$ ______

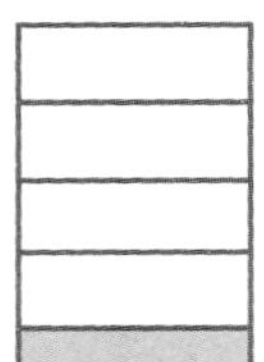
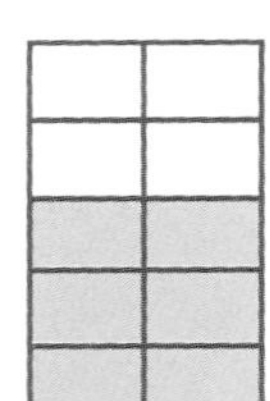
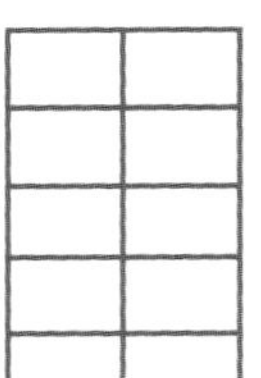

$\frac{1}{5} + \frac{6}{10} =$ ______

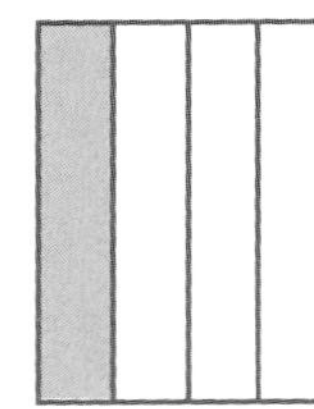
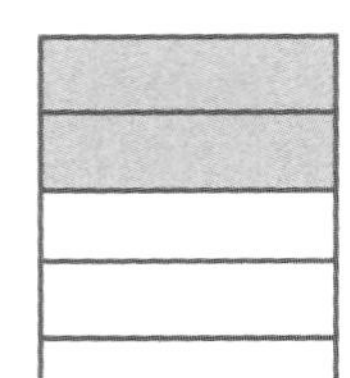
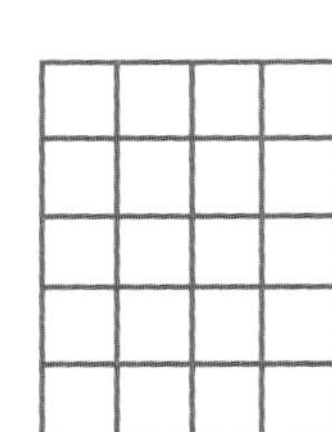

$\frac{1}{4} + \frac{2}{5} =$ ______

Adding fractions

Let's Learn!

When you add fractions with different denominators, try making equivalent fractions using the **least common denominator (LCD)**. The LCD is the smallest common multiple of both denominators. Try it for $\frac{1}{3} + \frac{2}{5}$.

To find the LCD of two fractions, write a few multiples of each denominator. Circle the smallest multiple they share. For this example, the LCD is 15.

Multiples of 3: 3, 6, 9, 12, (15)

Multiples of 5: 5, 10, (15,) 20, 25

Make equivalent fractions using the LCD as the denominator, and then add.

$$\frac{1}{3} + \frac{2}{5}$$

$$\downarrow \quad \downarrow$$

$$\frac{5}{15} + \frac{6}{15} = \frac{11}{15}$$

Add using the LCD. Write your answer in simplest form.

$\frac{1}{4} + \frac{1}{6} =$ $\frac{5}{12}$

$\downarrow \quad \downarrow$

$\frac{3}{12} + \frac{2}{12} = \frac{5}{12}$

$\frac{1}{5} + \frac{3}{10} =$ ______

$\frac{1}{2} + \frac{4}{9} =$ ______

$\frac{1}{4} + \frac{2}{3} =$ ______

IXL.com skill ID R7P

Adding fractions

Add. Write your answer in simplest form.

$\frac{1}{8} + \frac{3}{4} =$ $\frac{1}{8} + \frac{6}{8} = \frac{7}{8}$

$\frac{1}{7} + \frac{1}{14} =$ ______

$\frac{1}{15} + \frac{2}{5} =$ ______

$\frac{7}{12} + \frac{1}{4} =$ ______

$\frac{3}{8} + \frac{1}{3} =$ ______

$\frac{1}{5} + \frac{1}{3} =$ ______

$\frac{1}{6} + \frac{2}{3} =$ ______

$\frac{1}{2} + \frac{2}{9} =$ ______

$\frac{7}{18} + \frac{1}{6} =$ ______

$\frac{3}{4} + \frac{1}{16} =$ ______

Challenge yourself! Add. Write your answer in simplest form.

$\frac{1}{3} + \frac{1}{3} + \frac{1}{12} =$ ______

$\frac{1}{2} + \frac{3}{14} + \frac{1}{7} =$ ______

IXL.com
skill ID
D9N

Answer each question. Write your answer in simplest form.

Natalie is baking cookies for a bake sale. Of her cookies, $\frac{1}{2}$ are chocolate chip and $\frac{1}{3}$ are peanut butter. What fraction of the cookies are either chocolate chip or peanut butter? ________________

Chris sold pumpkins at the farmers' market. He sold $\frac{3}{7}$ of his pumpkins in the morning and $\frac{5}{14}$ of his pumpkins in the afternoon. What fraction of his pumpkins did Chris sell in all? ________________

Nora's Knitting Corner received a shipment of yarn today. In the shipment, $\frac{2}{3}$ of the yarn was blue and $\frac{1}{7}$ of the yarn was red. What fraction of the yarn was either blue or red? ________________

Out of Javier's shirts, $\frac{5}{12}$ are striped, $\frac{1}{3}$ are polka-dotted, and $\frac{1}{6}$ are plaid. The rest of his shirts have no designs at all. What total fraction of his shirts have designs? ________________

Subtracting fractions

Let's Learn!

To subtract fractions with different denominators, make equivalent fractions using the LCD. Then subtract. Try it for $\frac{1}{3} - \frac{1}{4}$.

$$\frac{1}{3} - \frac{1}{4}$$

$$\frac{4}{12} - \frac{3}{12} = \frac{1}{12}$$

Subtract. Write your answer in simplest form.

$\frac{1}{2} - \frac{1}{3} =$ $\frac{3}{6} - \frac{2}{6} = \frac{1}{6}$

$\frac{5}{9} - \frac{1}{3} =$ ______

$\frac{11}{12} - \frac{5}{6} =$ ______

$\frac{7}{8} - \frac{1}{2} =$ ______

$\frac{4}{5} - \frac{1}{2} =$ ______

$\frac{5}{12} - \frac{1}{4} =$ ______

$\frac{3}{10} - \frac{1}{5} =$ ______

$\frac{5}{7} - \frac{2}{3} =$ ______

$\frac{3}{4} - \frac{1}{3} =$ ______

$\frac{3}{11} - \frac{1}{5} =$ ______

Subtract. Write your answer in simplest form.

$\frac{2}{3} - \frac{1}{5} =$ ________________

$\frac{7}{8} - \frac{1}{3} =$ ________________

$\frac{13}{18} - \frac{1}{2} =$ ________________

$\frac{11}{14} - \frac{3}{7} =$ ________________

$\frac{1}{4} - \frac{1}{9} =$ ________________

$\frac{11}{12} - \frac{2}{5} =$ ________________

$\frac{9}{10} - \frac{2}{5} =$ ________________

$\frac{1}{2} - \frac{4}{9} =$ ________________

$\frac{2}{9} - \frac{1}{6} =$ ________________

$\frac{5}{6} - \frac{1}{11} =$ ________________

$\frac{11}{14} - \frac{1}{2} =$ ________________

$\frac{10}{11} - \frac{1}{2} =$ ________________

20 Word problems

Answer each question. Write your answer in simplest form.

A nature trail is $\frac{7}{10}$ of a mile long. Lola has walked $\frac{1}{5}$ of a mile so far. How many miles does she have left? ____________

Tyler had $\frac{3}{4}$ of a quart of lemonade. He poured $\frac{1}{2}$ of a quart into a large glass. How many quarts of lemonade does Tyler have left? ____________

Brooke's hot cocoa recipe uses $\frac{2}{3}$ of a cup of white sugar and $\frac{1}{4}$ of a cup of cocoa powder. How much more white sugar than cocoa powder does she need? ____________

Philip brings $\frac{7}{8}$ of a pound of almonds on a hike with his friends. He gives $\frac{1}{3}$ of a pound to Nicole and $\frac{1}{4}$ of a pound to Amaya. How many pounds of almonds does he have left? ____________

IXL.com skill ID **TCD**

Let's review! Add or subtract. Write your answer in simplest form.

$\frac{1}{9} + \frac{1}{3} =$ ______________

$\frac{11}{12} - \frac{1}{3} =$ ______________

$\frac{7}{8} - \frac{1}{4} =$ ______________

$\frac{1}{8} + \frac{1}{16} =$ ______________

$\frac{17}{18} - \frac{1}{6} =$ ______________

$\frac{2}{3} - \frac{5}{18} =$ ______________

$\frac{1}{2} + \frac{5}{14} =$ ______________

$\frac{7}{10} + \frac{1}{4} =$ ______________

$\frac{2}{11} + \frac{1}{9} =$ ______________

$\frac{6}{7} - \frac{3}{14} =$ ______________

$\frac{13}{15} - \frac{2}{3} =$ ______________

$\frac{7}{12} - \frac{3}{8} =$ ______________

22 Adding and subtracting fractions

Add or subtract. Draw a line between the equivalent answers.

$\frac{1}{5} + \frac{1}{2} = \frac{7}{10}$

$\frac{1}{2} + \frac{1}{6}$

$\frac{1}{4} + \frac{2}{5}$

$\frac{1}{6} + \frac{1}{4}$

$\frac{1}{4} + \frac{1}{8}$

$\frac{2}{9} + \frac{1}{3}$

$\frac{3}{4} - \frac{1}{10}$

$\frac{5}{6} - \frac{5}{12}$

$\frac{4}{5} - \frac{1}{10} = \frac{7}{10}$

$\frac{13}{15} - \frac{1}{5}$

$\frac{5}{6} - \frac{5}{18}$

$\frac{7}{8} - \frac{1}{2}$

IXL.com
skill ID
N6D

Follow the path!

If you land on an answer that is greater than $\frac{1}{2}$, go to the right one square.

If you land on an answer that is less than $\frac{1}{2}$, go to the left one square.

If you land on an answer that is equal to $\frac{1}{2}$, go down one square.

START ↓

$\frac{1}{2} + \frac{2}{5}$	$\frac{7}{8} - \frac{1}{6}$	$\frac{1}{6} + \frac{1}{3}$	$\frac{1}{2} + \frac{1}{5}$	$\frac{3}{4} - \frac{1}{2}$
$\frac{8}{9} - \frac{1}{18}$	$\frac{1}{8} + \frac{3}{8}$	$\frac{3}{4} - \frac{2}{3}$	$\frac{1}{3} + \frac{5}{9}$	$\frac{2}{5} - \frac{1}{4}$
$\frac{3}{14} + \frac{1}{2}$	$\frac{9}{14} - \frac{1}{7}$	$\frac{1}{9} + \frac{1}{3}$	$\frac{1}{3} + \frac{1}{6}$	$\frac{1}{5} + \frac{2}{3}$
$\frac{1}{3} + \frac{1}{5}$	$\frac{3}{5} + \frac{2}{9}$	$\frac{3}{4} + \frac{2}{11}$	$\frac{5}{9} - \frac{1}{18}$	$\frac{5}{14} + \frac{1}{7}$
$\frac{6}{7} - \frac{1}{14}$	$\frac{3}{5} + \frac{1}{5}$	$\frac{5}{6} - \frac{1}{9}$	$\frac{1}{4} + \frac{1}{4}$	$\frac{1}{5} + \frac{4}{5}$

FINISH ↓

IXL.com
skill ID
9JR

Adding and subtracting fractions

Add or subtract. Write your answer in simplest form.

$\frac{7}{10} - \frac{9}{20} =$ ______

$\frac{5}{24} + \frac{17}{48} =$ ______

$\frac{33}{64} - \frac{5}{32} =$ ______

$\frac{6}{25} + \frac{8}{75} =$ ______

$\frac{3}{4} - \frac{21}{40} =$ ______

$\frac{20}{27} - \frac{4}{81} =$ ______

$\frac{1}{2} + \frac{2}{15} =$ ______

$\frac{5}{16} + \frac{7}{12} =$ ______

$\frac{17}{30} - \frac{7}{15} =$ ______

$\frac{7}{100} - \frac{3}{50} =$ ______

$\frac{9}{16} - \frac{1}{12} =$ ______

$\frac{4}{25} - \frac{7}{75} =$ ______

$\frac{1}{27} + \frac{25}{54} =$ ______

Write the mixed number shown.

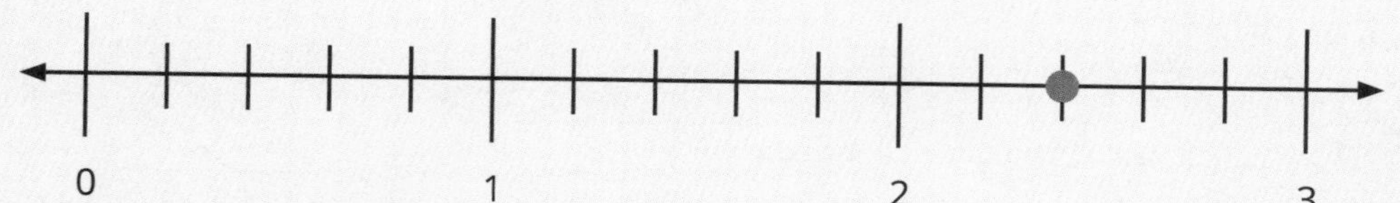

$2\frac{2}{5}$ ____________

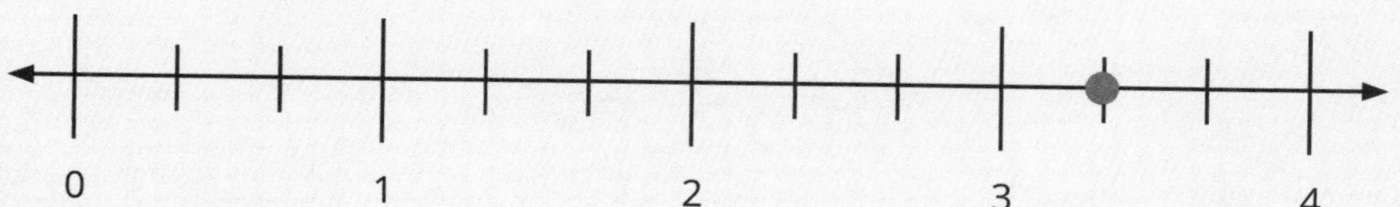

____

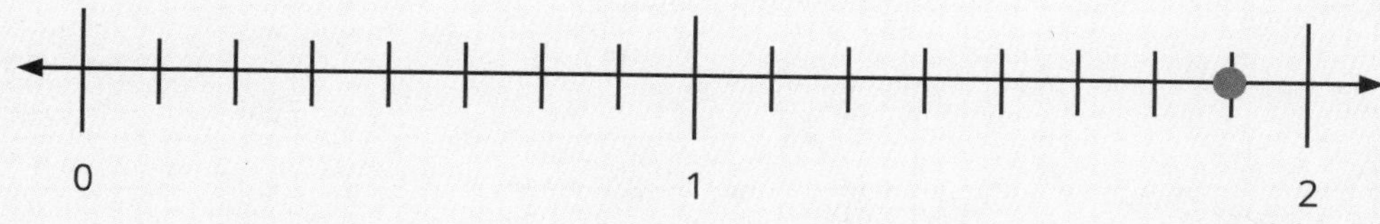

____

Show each mixed number on the number line.

$1\frac{2}{3}$

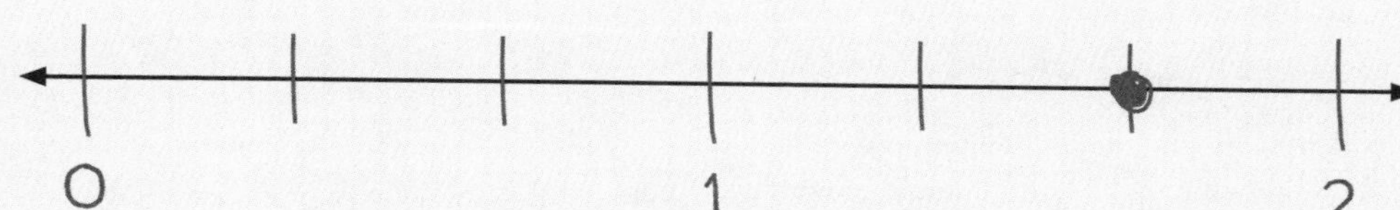

$1\frac{1}{5}$

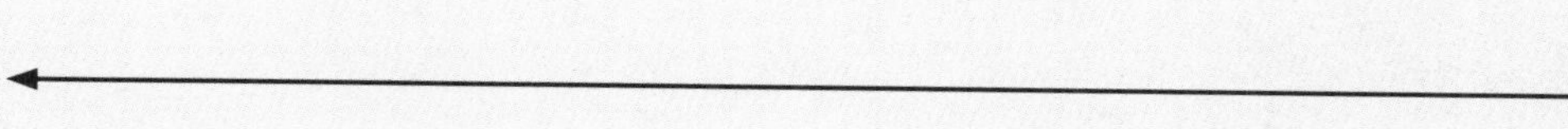

$2\frac{1}{2}$

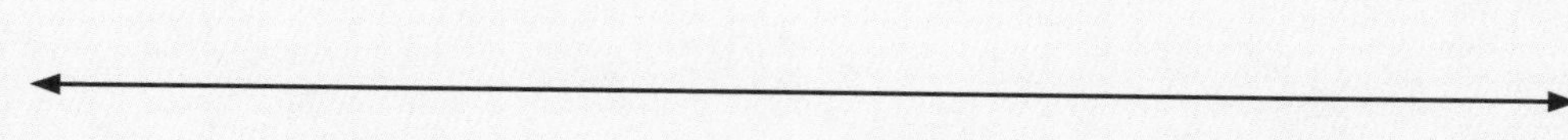

Mixed numbers and improper fractions

Write each amount as a mixed number and an improper fraction.

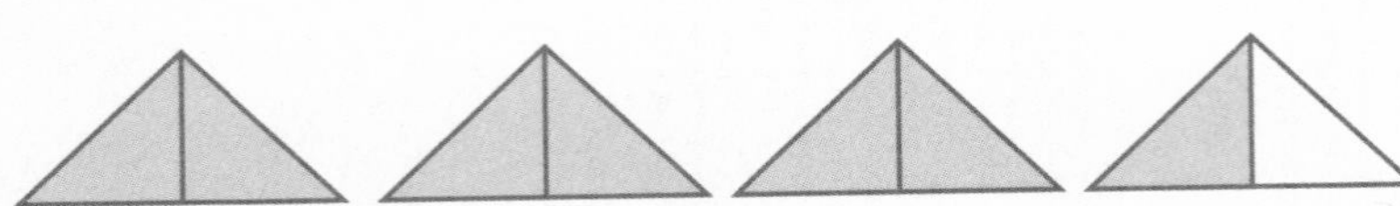

$3\frac{1}{2}$ = $\frac{7}{2}$

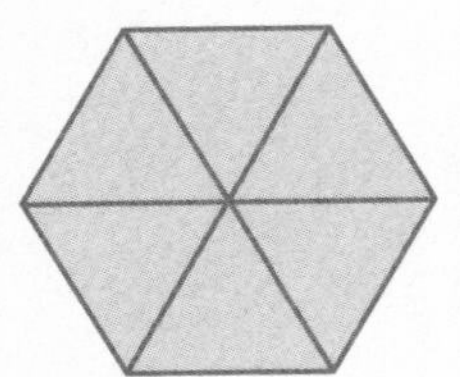
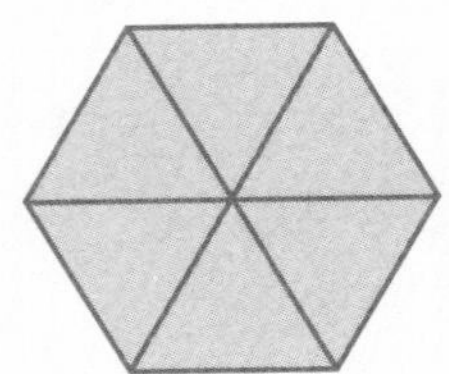
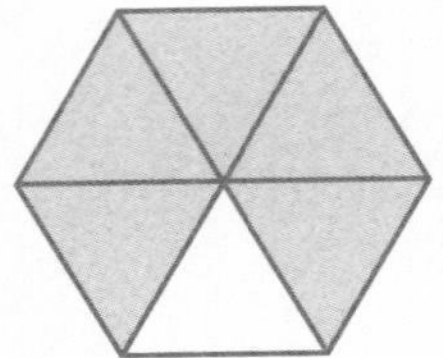

______ = ______

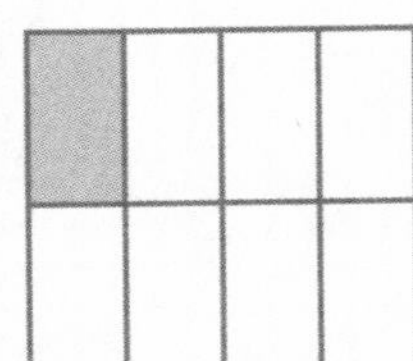

______ = ______

Write the missing improper fraction or mixed number. Draw models to help.

$2\frac{1}{3}$ = $\frac{7}{3}$

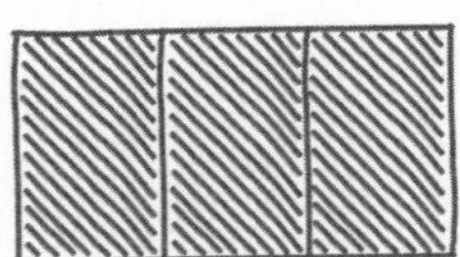
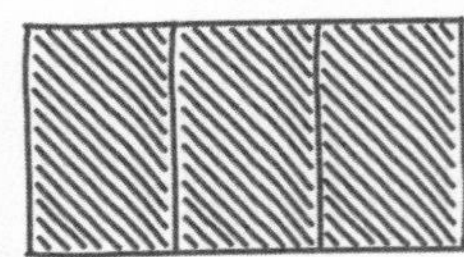
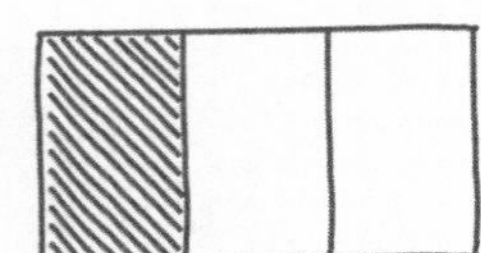

______ = $\frac{13}{4}$

$1\frac{3}{5}$ = ______

Write the mixed numbers as improper fractions.

$1\frac{1}{2}$ = $\frac{3}{2}$ $3\frac{2}{4}$ = ______ $2\frac{1}{7}$ = ______

$1\frac{4}{6}$ = ______ $3\frac{3}{10}$ = ______ $3\frac{1}{6}$ = ______

$2\frac{2}{5}$ = ______ $3\frac{6}{7}$ = ______ $1\frac{7}{8}$ = ______

$2\frac{5}{9}$ = ______ $1\frac{1}{11}$ = ______ $4\frac{1}{12}$ = ______

FIND THE RULE! Can you come up with a rule for converting mixed numbers to improper fractions?

Mixed numbers and improper fractions

Write the improper fractions as mixed numbers in simplest form.

$\frac{6}{4}$ = $1\frac{2}{4} = 1\frac{1}{2}$

$\frac{11}{6}$ = ____________

$\frac{9}{2}$ = ____________

$\frac{22}{8}$ = ____________

$\frac{16}{9}$ = ____________

$\frac{18}{4}$ = ____________

$\frac{34}{8}$ = ____________

$\frac{36}{7}$ = ____________

$\frac{16}{12}$ = ____________

$\frac{31}{11}$ = ____________

KEEP IT GOING! Can you come up with a rule for converting improper fractions to mixed numbers?

Draw a line from the improper fraction to the equivalent mixed number in simplest form.

Improper fraction	Mixed number
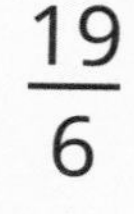 $\frac{19}{6}$	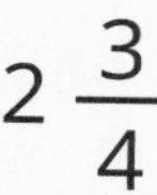 $2\frac{3}{4}$
$\frac{11}{4}$	$1\frac{2}{3}$
$\frac{20}{12}$	$2\frac{1}{4}$
$\frac{22}{10}$	$2\frac{1}{5}$
$\frac{41}{12}$	$3\frac{2}{3}$
$\frac{18}{8}$	$3\frac{1}{6}$
$\frac{33}{9}$	$3\frac{5}{12}$

IXL.com
skill ID
B7X

Adding mixed numbers

Let's Learn!

You can add mixed numbers by first adding the whole numbers and then adding the fractions. Try it with $2\frac{1}{3} + 3\frac{1}{9}$.

$2 + 3 = 5$ Add the whole numbers first.

$\frac{1}{3} + \frac{1}{9}$

Next, add the fractions using the LCD.

$\frac{3}{9} + \frac{1}{9} = \frac{4}{9}$

$2\frac{1}{3} + 3\frac{1}{9} = 5\frac{4}{9}$ Combine these two answers to get the sum.

Add. Write your answer as a mixed number in simplest form.

$1\frac{1}{2} + 2\frac{1}{6} =$ $3\frac{2}{3}$

$1\frac{3}{6} + 2\frac{1}{6} = 3\frac{4}{6} = 3\frac{2}{3}$

$\frac{2}{9} + 4\frac{1}{9} =$ ______

$1\frac{1}{6} + 6\frac{7}{12} =$ ______

$7\frac{1}{5} + 3\frac{1}{2} =$ ______

$9\frac{3}{4} + \frac{1}{8} =$ ______

$6\frac{1}{4} + 8\frac{2}{3} =$ ______

Let's Learn!

When you add mixed numbers, the fraction in the sum might be improper. If this happens, you'll have to regroup! Try it with $4\frac{3}{4} + 2\frac{1}{2}$.

$4\frac{3}{4} + 2\frac{1}{2} = 6\frac{5}{4}$ Add the whole numbers. Then add the fractions using the LCD. The fraction in the sum, $\frac{5}{4}$, is improper.

$\frac{5}{4} = 1\frac{1}{4}$ Change the improper fraction into a mixed number.

$6 + 1\frac{1}{4} = 7\frac{1}{4}$ Add the whole numbers again to get the sum.

Add. Write your answer as a mixed number in simplest form.

$2\frac{2}{3} + 2\frac{1}{2} = 5\frac{1}{6}$

$2\frac{4}{6} + 2\frac{3}{6} = 4\frac{7}{6} = 5\frac{1}{6}$

$1\frac{7}{12} + 4\frac{5}{6} =$ ______

$7\frac{5}{7} + \frac{11}{14} =$ ______

$10\frac{4}{5} + 1\frac{1}{2} =$ ______

$6\frac{3}{4} + 1\frac{7}{10} =$ ______

$9\frac{1}{3} + \frac{4}{5} =$ ______

Adding mixed numbers

Add. Write your answer as a mixed number in simplest form.

$1\frac{5}{8} + 3\frac{7}{12} =$ ______

$3\frac{1}{7} + 7\frac{1}{2} =$ ______

$5\frac{7}{9} + 2\frac{5}{9} =$ ______

$7\frac{2}{3} + 1\frac{7}{8} =$ ______

$4\frac{3}{5} + 3\frac{5}{6} =$ ______

$9\frac{3}{4} + 1\frac{4}{5} =$ ______

Challenge yourself! Write your answer as a mixed number in simplest form.

$2\frac{1}{3} + 3\frac{1}{3} + 2\frac{11}{12} =$ ______

$7\frac{1}{4} + 1\frac{7}{8} + 1\frac{1}{2} =$ ______

IXL.com skill ID FHD

$1\frac{2}{3} + 2\frac{3}{4} + 6\frac{5}{6} =$ ______

Answer each question. Write your answer as a mixed number in simplest form.

Keenan spent the day trying out two new cupcake recipes. He used $2\frac{1}{3}$ cups of flour for the first recipe and 2 cups of flour for the second. How many cups of flour did Keenan use in all? ________________

Miles practiced the trumpet for $1\frac{1}{2}$ hours. Later, he practiced the drums for $1\frac{3}{4}$ hours. How long did Miles practice in total? ________________

It is Lila's job to feed the cats and dogs at the animal shelter. Each day she gives $4\frac{3}{4}$ pounds of food to the dogs and $3\frac{7}{8}$ pounds of food to the cats. How many pounds of food does she give the cats and dogs each day? ________________

At track practice, Stacy ran $1\frac{1}{2}$ laps to warm up. Then she ran $5\frac{7}{8}$ laps during her workout. She ran another $\frac{3}{4}$ of a lap to cool down. How many laps did she run in all? ________________

Subtracting mixed numbers

Let's Learn!

You can subtract mixed numbers by first subtracting the whole numbers and then subtracting the fractions. Try it with $3\frac{1}{6} - 2\frac{1}{12}$.

$3 - 2 = 1$ Subtract the whole numbers first.

$\frac{1}{6} - \frac{1}{12}$

$\downarrow \quad \downarrow$

$\frac{2}{12} - \frac{1}{12} = \frac{1}{12}$ Next, subtract the fractions using the LCD.

$3\frac{1}{6} - 2\frac{1}{12} = 1\frac{1}{12}$ Combine these answers to get the difference.

Subtract. Write your answer as a mixed number in simplest form.

$5\frac{1}{4} - 2\frac{1}{8} =$ $3\frac{1}{8}$

$5\frac{2}{8} - 2\frac{1}{8} = 3\frac{1}{8}$

$9\frac{3}{4} - 4\frac{1}{4} =$ ______

$7\frac{11}{12} - 3\frac{2}{3} =$ ______

$8\frac{4}{5} - 1\frac{1}{2} =$ ______

$11\frac{1}{2} - 6\frac{1}{7} =$ ______

$9\frac{7}{10} - 8\frac{1}{5} =$ ______

Let's Learn!

When you subtract mixed numbers, you may need to regroup. Try it with $3\frac{1}{4} - 1\frac{5}{8}$. First, use equivalent fractions to get the same denominator. Rewrite the problem as $3\frac{2}{8} - 1\frac{5}{8}$.

$3\frac{2}{8} - 1\frac{5}{8}$ — You can't subtract $\frac{2}{8} - \frac{5}{8}$. So, you'll need to regroup $3\frac{2}{8}$.

$3\frac{2}{8} = 2\frac{8}{8} + \frac{2}{8} = 2\frac{10}{8}$ — You can regroup one whole in $3\frac{2}{8}$ to get $2\frac{10}{8}$.

$2\frac{10}{8} - 1\frac{5}{8} = 1\frac{5}{8}$ — Now you can subtract!

Subtract. Write your answer as a mixed number in simplest form.

$4\frac{1}{4} - 1\frac{1}{2} =$ $2\frac{3}{4}$

$4\frac{1}{4} - 1\frac{2}{4} = 3\frac{5}{4} - 1\frac{2}{4} = 2\frac{3}{4}$

$3\frac{1}{3} - 1\frac{5}{9} =$ ______

$6\frac{1}{12} - 4\frac{3}{4} =$ ______

$5\frac{1}{6} - 3\frac{3}{4} =$ ______

$11 - 4\frac{7}{8} =$ ______

$12\frac{1}{3} - \frac{5}{7} =$ ______

Subtracting mixed numbers

Subtract. Write your answer as a mixed number in simplest form.

$4\frac{1}{8} - \frac{1}{2} =$ ______

$7\frac{3}{4} - 3\frac{5}{6} =$ ______

$8\frac{1}{5} - 3\frac{6}{7} =$ ______

$5 - 2\frac{6}{7} =$ ______

$11\frac{1}{4} - 9\frac{1}{2} =$ ______

$3\frac{2}{5} - 1\frac{5}{6} =$ ______

$8\frac{3}{8} - 4\frac{5}{6} =$ ______

$5\frac{5}{18} - 2\frac{7}{9} =$ ______

$12 - 1\frac{7}{12} =$ ______

Answer each question. Write your answer as a mixed number in simplest form.

Liza bought a rope that was $6\frac{1}{3}$ yards long. She cut off $5\frac{1}{6}$ yards to make a tire swing. How much rope does Liza have left? __________

Mandy had 5 pizzas to share with her friends at a sleepover. They ate $3\frac{1}{8}$ pizzas. How much pizza was left? __________

Jason and his friends are having a $4\frac{1}{2}$-hour-long movie marathon. They have watched for $1\frac{5}{6}$ hours so far. How many hours are left of the marathon? __________

The hike from Terry's house to the beach is $9\frac{2}{5}$ miles long. Terry has only $1\frac{7}{10}$ miles left of the hike. How many miles has he already hiked?

____

Addition and subtraction review

Time to review! Add or subtract. Write your answer as a proper fraction or mixed number in simplest form.

$\frac{2}{5} - \frac{1}{3} =$ ______

$3\frac{7}{12} + 2\frac{1}{6} =$ ______

$7\frac{3}{4} - 5\frac{2}{7} =$ ______

$\frac{4}{5} + \frac{9}{10} =$ ______

$\frac{4}{11} + 7\frac{1}{2} =$ ______

$4\frac{1}{8} - 2\frac{2}{3} =$ ______

$3\frac{1}{4} + \frac{7}{9} =$ ______

$\frac{6}{7} + \frac{1}{3} =$ ______

$8 - \frac{5}{7} =$ ______

$2\frac{3}{5} + 3\frac{1}{7} =$ ______

$4 - 1\frac{11}{12} =$ ______

$\frac{5}{6} - \frac{2}{9} =$ ______

Add or subtract to follow each path! Write your answers as proper fractions or mixed numbers in simplest form.

$\frac{7}{8}$	$-\frac{5}{12}$ →	$\frac{11}{24}$
$+\frac{1}{4}$ ↑		$+\frac{2}{3}$ ↓
$\frac{5}{8}$	← $-\frac{1}{2}$	$1\frac{1}{8}$

$1\frac{1}{3}$	$+\frac{1}{2}$ →	
$-1\frac{7}{12}$ ↑		$+1\frac{1}{3}$ ↓
	← $-\frac{1}{4}$	

$7\frac{1}{8}$	$-5\frac{1}{2}$ →	
$+\frac{1}{4}$ ↑		$+\frac{3}{4}$ ↓
	← $+4\frac{1}{2}$	

	$-3\frac{1}{3}$ →	
$-\frac{7}{9}$ ↑		$-\frac{5}{9}$ ↓
	← $+4\frac{2}{3}$	$\frac{2}{3}$

IXL.com skill ID **PBF**

40 Comparing sums and differences

Add or subtract. Compare each pair using >, <, or =.

$\frac{1}{2} + \frac{1}{4} \; (>) \; \frac{1}{3} + \frac{1}{6}$

$\frac{3}{4} > \frac{3}{6}$

$\frac{4}{5} + \frac{1}{2} \; \bigcirc \; 2\frac{7}{10} - 1\frac{2}{5}$

$\frac{5}{8} - \frac{1}{2} \; \bigcirc \; \frac{1}{4} + \frac{1}{8}$

$3\frac{3}{4} + 5\frac{1}{3} \; \bigcirc \; 10 - 1\frac{7}{12}$

$\frac{11}{12} + \frac{1}{4} \; \bigcirc \; 1\frac{5}{12} - \frac{2}{3}$

$\frac{1}{7} + \frac{3}{4} \; \bigcirc \; \frac{5}{6} + \frac{4}{5}$

$\frac{7}{8} + \frac{3}{4} \; \bigcirc \; 3 - 2\frac{1}{4}$

$8\frac{1}{6} - 4\frac{11}{12} \; \bigcirc \; 5\frac{3}{10} - 2\frac{2}{5}$

$2\frac{8}{9} + 1\frac{5}{6} \; \bigcirc \; 6\frac{1}{4} - 1\frac{7}{8}$

IXL.com
skill ID
9GK

Circle all of the problems that have answers greater than $\frac{1}{4}$.

$\frac{1}{8} + \frac{1}{4}$ $\qquad$ $\frac{1}{2} - \frac{1}{4}$ $\qquad$ $1\frac{1}{4} - 1\frac{1}{8}$

Circle all of the problems that have answers greater than $\frac{1}{2}$.

$\frac{3}{8} + \frac{1}{6}$ $\qquad$ $1\frac{1}{9} - \frac{1}{2}$ $\qquad$ $2\frac{3}{4} - 2\frac{1}{3}$

Circle all of the problems that have answers greater than 1.

$\frac{3}{4} + \frac{1}{3}$ $\qquad$ $3\frac{3}{5} - 2\frac{5}{7}$ $\qquad$ $\frac{1}{5} + \frac{7}{9}$

Circle all of the problems that have answers greater than $1\frac{1}{2}$.

$5 - 3\frac{3}{4}$ $\qquad$ $\frac{3}{4} + \frac{7}{8}$ $\qquad$ $7\frac{1}{4} - 5\frac{2}{3}$

Equations

Solve each equation. Use the LCD to help! Write your answer as a proper fraction or mixed number in simplest form.

$$\frac{11}{14} = p + \frac{4}{7} \quad \frac{8}{14}$$

$p = \frac{3}{14}$

$$n = \frac{2}{3} + \frac{4}{5}$$

$n =$ ______

$$a = 4\frac{1}{2} + 1\frac{3}{4}$$

$a =$ ______

$$r - \frac{1}{9} = \frac{1}{18}$$

$r =$ ______

$$5\frac{1}{3} = 5\frac{2}{3} - y$$

$y =$ ______

$$1\frac{1}{6} = 4\frac{7}{12} - m$$

$m =$ ______

$$2\frac{1}{2} + k = 2\frac{5}{8}$$

$k =$ ______

Answer each question. Write your answer as a proper fraction or mixed number in simplest form.

If you add me to $\frac{1}{2}$, you get $\frac{7}{12}$. What number am I?

If you subtract $\frac{3}{8}$ from me, you will have $\frac{3}{8}$. What number am I?

If you add $1\frac{1}{2}$ to me, you will have $2\frac{5}{6}$. What number am I?

If you subtract $\frac{1}{10}$ from me, you will have $3\frac{1}{2}$. What number am I?

If you add me to $1\frac{2}{3}$, you get $3\frac{1}{6}$. What number am I?

Use the rule to fill in the missing numbers. Write each number as a proper fraction or mixed number in simplest form.

Rule: add $\frac{3}{4}$	2	$2\frac{3}{4}$	$3\frac{1}{2}$	$4\frac{1}{4}$	5

Rule: subtract $\frac{3}{8}$	$9\frac{1}{4}$	$8\frac{7}{8}$		$8\frac{1}{8}$	

Rule: add $2\frac{1}{5}$	$\frac{3}{10}$		$4\frac{7}{10}$		$9\frac{1}{10}$

Rule: subtract $\frac{1}{3}$	$2\frac{5}{6}$	$2\frac{1}{2}$			$1\frac{1}{2}$

Challenge yourself! Find the rule using the LCD. Then fill in the missing numbers.

Rule: ADD $\frac{1}{10}$	$\frac{7}{10}$	$\frac{4}{5}$	$\frac{9}{10}$	1	$1\frac{1}{10}$	$1\frac{1}{5}$

Rule:	$7\frac{3}{4}$	$7\frac{1}{2}$		7	$6\frac{3}{4}$	

IXL.com skill ID **MMR**

Answer each question. Write your answer as a proper fraction or mixed number in simplest form.

Samuel bought three different colors of balloons for his sister's graduation party. Out of the balloons, $\frac{1}{6}$ were red, $\frac{5}{8}$ were yellow, and the rest were orange. What fraction of the balloons were either red or yellow? __________

In Esteban's piggy bank, $\frac{1}{3}$ of the coins are quarters and $\frac{3}{10}$ are dimes. What fraction of the coins in Esteban's piggy bank are either quarters or dimes? __________

John had $3\frac{2}{3}$ loaves of bread. He used $1\frac{5}{6}$ loaves to make sandwiches for his family. How many loaves of bread did John have left? __________

Alyssa has $1\frac{1}{4}$ inches of twine and needs more to make a bracelet. She buys $8\frac{1}{2}$ inches more and makes a bracelet that uses $5\frac{3}{4}$ inches of twine. How much twine does she have left? __________

46 Word problems

Answer each question. Write your answer as a proper fraction or mixed number in simplest form.

Marcela wanted to go on two hikes during her camping trip. She planned out her hikes on this piece of paper:

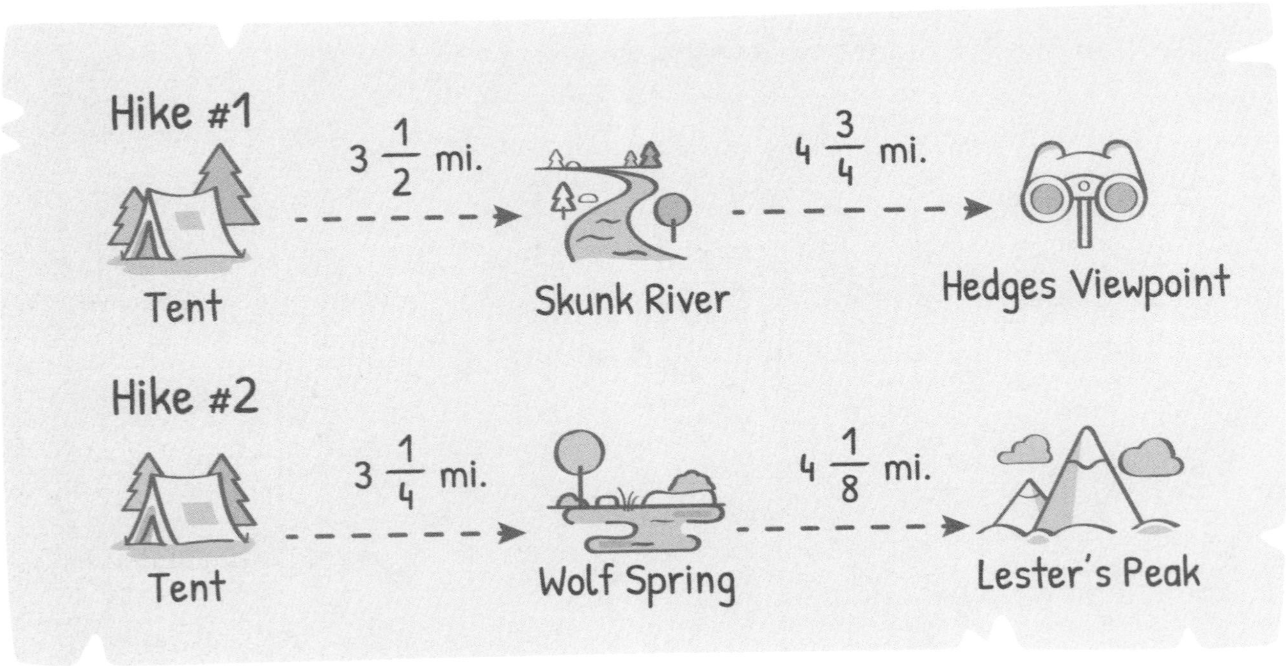

Hike #1

Tent — $3\frac{1}{2}$ mi. → Skunk River — $4\frac{3}{4}$ mi. → Hedges Viewpoint

Hike #2

Tent — $3\frac{1}{4}$ mi. → Wolf Spring — $4\frac{1}{8}$ mi. → Lester's Peak

How long is the hike to Hedges Viewpoint? ____________

How long is the hike to Lester's Peak? ____________

How much longer is the hike to Hedges Viewpoint than the hike to Lester's Peak? ____________

How much longer is the path from Skunk River to Hedges Viewpoint than the path from Wolf Spring to Lester's Peak? ____________

Let's Learn!

You can multiply fractions by whole numbers using models. Try it for $3 \times \frac{1}{7}$.

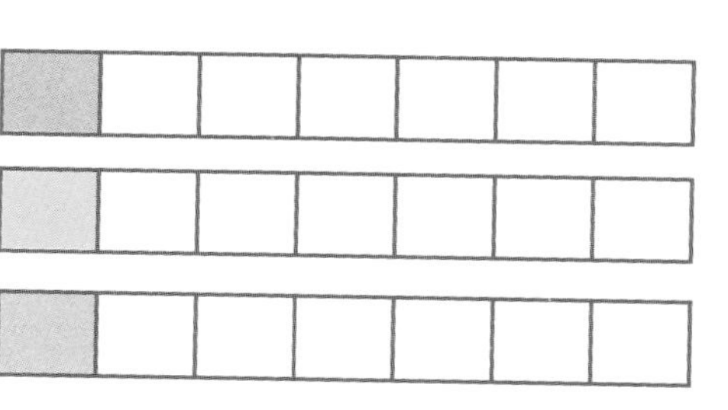

$3 \times \frac{1}{7}$

$3 \times \frac{1}{7} = \frac{3}{7}$

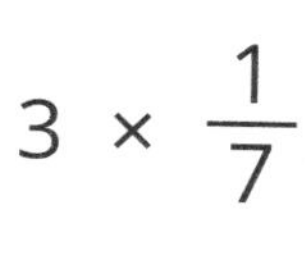

Complete the multiplication sentence for each model. Write your answer in simplest form.

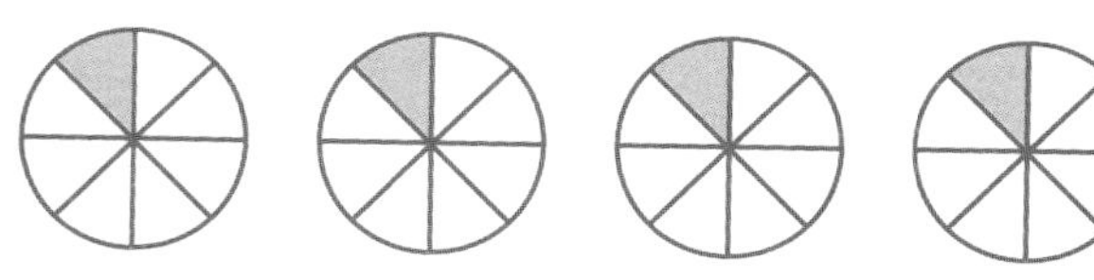

$\underline{4} \times \underline{\frac{1}{8}} = \underline{\frac{4}{8} = \frac{1}{2}}$

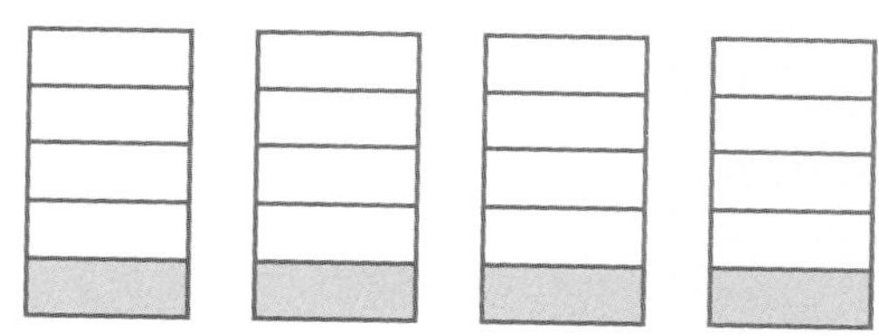

_____ × _____ = _________

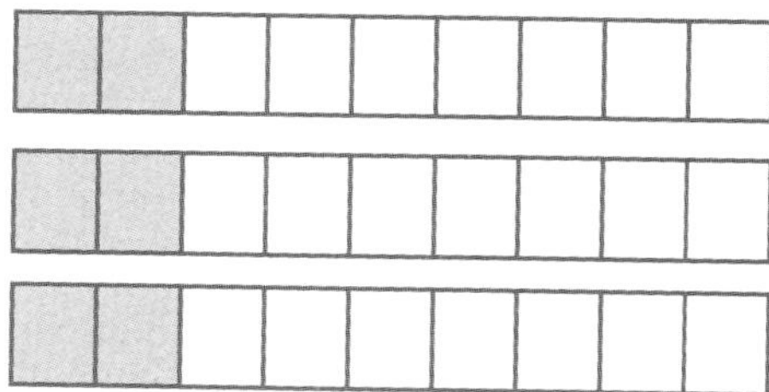

_____ × _____ = _________

_____ × _____ = _________

IXL.com
skill ID
VXF

Multiplying a whole number by a fraction

Let's Learn!

You can multiply fractions by whole numbers without using models. Just multiply the whole number by the numerator and keep the denominator the same. Try it with $2 \times \frac{3}{7}$.

$$2 \times \frac{3}{7} = \frac{2 \times 3}{7} = \frac{6}{7}$$

Multiply. Write your answer as a proper fraction or mixed number in simplest form.

$4 \times \frac{1}{10} = \frac{4}{10} = \frac{2}{5}$

$10 \times \frac{1}{7} =$ ________

$\frac{1}{3} \times 8 =$ ________

$1 \times \frac{4}{9} =$ ________

$\frac{4}{5} \times 6 =$ ________

$\frac{3}{4} \times 3 =$ ________

$2 \times \frac{1}{8} =$ ________

$11 \times \frac{4}{11} =$ ________

$7 \times \frac{3}{5} =$ ________

$\frac{5}{8} \times 4 =$ ________

IXL.com
skill ID
QFQ

Multiply. Write your answer as a proper fraction or mixed number in simplest form.

$\frac{2}{3} \times 7 =$ ______

$6 \times \frac{1}{2} =$ ______

$11 \times \frac{3}{4} =$ ______

$\frac{5}{6} \times 4 =$ ______

$7 \times \frac{1}{5} =$ ______

$2 \times \frac{4}{9} =$ ______

$5 \times \frac{1}{3} =$ ______

$8 \times \frac{3}{8} =$ ______

$\frac{2}{3} \times 3 =$ ______

$\frac{5}{12} \times 7 =$ ______

Challenge yourself! Multiply. Write your answer as a proper fraction or mixed number in simplest form.

$\frac{3}{5} \times 15 =$ ______

$16 \times \frac{2}{9} =$ ______

$20 \times \frac{4}{7} =$ ______

$\frac{2}{3} \times 17 =$ ______

IXL.com
skill ID
K69

Multiplying a whole number by a fraction

Fill in the missing numbers.

$\frac{5}{11} \times 9 = \frac{45}{\square}$

$\frac{\square}{4} \times 7 = \frac{21}{4}$

$\square \times \frac{5}{6} = \frac{25}{6}$

$2 \times \frac{\square}{8} = \frac{6}{8}$

$\frac{2}{9} \times \square = \frac{16}{9}$

$\frac{3}{4} \times \square = \frac{12}{4}$

$8 \times \frac{6}{7} = \frac{\square}{7}$

$\square \times \frac{4}{5} = \frac{24}{5}$

$7 \times \frac{\square}{10} = \frac{21}{10}$

$\frac{\square}{11} \times 9 = \frac{36}{11}$

DIG DEEPER! Can you write each of the products on this page as a proper fraction or mixed number in simplest form?

Let's Learn!

If you have a **fraction of a number**, you can multiply to find that amount.

$$\frac{1}{3} \text{ of } 9 = \frac{1}{3} \times 9 = 3$$

Multiply. Write your answer as a proper fraction or mixed number in simplest form.

$\frac{2}{3}$ of 12 = ________

$\frac{1}{4}$ of 3 = ________

$\frac{1}{2}$ of 14 = ________

$\frac{5}{7}$ of 9 = ________

$\frac{1}{5}$ of 11 = ________

$\frac{2}{3}$ of 10 = ________

$\frac{3}{4}$ of 4 = ________

$\frac{1}{8}$ of 7 = ________

$\frac{1}{6}$ of 11 = ________

IXL.com skill ID AHX

Word problems

Multiply. Write your answer as a proper fraction or mixed number in simplest form.

A group of 8 friends were having a picnic, and $\frac{3}{4}$ of them brought sandwiches. How many of the friends brought a sandwich? ________________

A bike trail is 12 miles, and $\frac{5}{6}$ of it goes along the river. How many miles of the trail are along the river? ________________

Rebecca has 9 video games on her shelf, and $\frac{1}{3}$ of them are racing games. How many racing games does Rebecca have? ________________

A group of 10 friends went to a ski resort, but $\frac{2}{5}$ of them did not know how to ski. How many friends did not know how to ski? ________________

Answer each question. Write your answer as a proper fraction or mixed number in simplest form.

Eliza is making salsa and fruit salad for a large family reunion. She has a recipe for both dishes, but she'll need to **triple** the salsa recipe and **quadruple** the fruit salad recipe to have enough for everyone.

Fruit Salad Recipe

2 cups strawberries
1/2 tsp. lime juice
2/3 cup orange juice
3 bananas
2 oranges
1/2 cup grapes

How many onions will Eliza need for the salsa? __________

How much orange juice will Eliza need for the fruit salad? __________

How much salt will she put in the salsa? __________

How much lime juice will Eliza need to make both recipes?

____

Multiplying fractions

Let's Learn!

To multiply two fractions, multiply the numerators and multiply the denominators.

$$\frac{3}{5} \times \frac{1}{4} = \frac{3 \times 1}{5 \times 4} = \frac{3}{20}$$

Multiply. Write your answer in simplest form.

$\frac{2}{3} \times \frac{1}{2} =$ $\frac{2}{6} = \frac{1}{3}$

$\frac{7}{12} \times \frac{1}{2} =$ __________

$\frac{1}{4} \times \frac{3}{4} =$ __________

$\frac{7}{8} \times \frac{2}{3} =$ __________

$\frac{1}{3} \times \frac{4}{9} =$ __________

$\frac{1}{12} \times \frac{1}{4} =$ __________

$\frac{1}{8} \times \frac{5}{6} =$ __________

$\frac{1}{6} \times \frac{3}{4} =$ __________

$\frac{7}{10} \times \frac{3}{8} =$ __________

$\frac{3}{11} \times \frac{1}{3} =$ __________

$\frac{7}{10} \times \frac{4}{5} =$ __________

IXL.com
skill ID
8KV

Multiply. Write your answer in simplest form.

$\frac{2}{5} \times \frac{1}{3} =$ ______

$\frac{9}{10} \times \frac{3}{4} =$ ______

$\frac{3}{10} \times \frac{1}{2} =$ ______

$\frac{2}{11} \times \frac{1}{5} =$ ______

$\frac{5}{6} \times \frac{2}{7} =$ ______

$\frac{5}{7} \times \frac{1}{8} =$ ______

$\frac{5}{8} \times \frac{1}{3} =$ ______

$\frac{3}{5} \times \frac{1}{4} =$ ______

$\frac{8}{9} \times \frac{2}{9} =$ ______

$\frac{4}{5} \times \frac{5}{12} =$ ______

$\frac{1}{5} \times \frac{3}{4} =$ ______

$\frac{9}{10} \times \frac{1}{2} =$ ______

LOOK AGAIN! There are three problems on this page with the same answer. Can you find them?

IXL.com skill ID **S6G**

Fractions of a fraction

Let's Learn!

To find a **fraction of a fraction**, you can multiply! For example, to find $\frac{1}{4}$ of $\frac{1}{2}$, multiply those two fractions together.

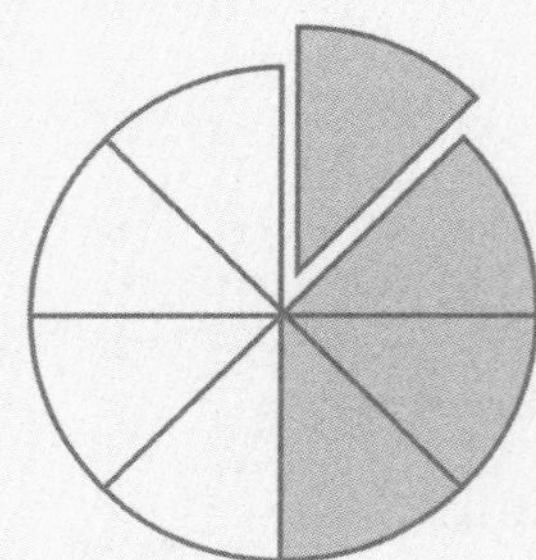

$$\frac{1}{4} \times \frac{1}{2} = \frac{1}{8}$$

Multiply. Write your answer in simplest form.

$\frac{1}{3}$ of $\frac{4}{5}$ = __________

$\frac{2}{3}$ of $\frac{1}{4}$ = __________

$\frac{3}{5}$ of $\frac{3}{7}$ = __________

$\frac{5}{9}$ of $\frac{5}{6}$ = __________

$\frac{2}{7}$ of $\frac{1}{4}$ = __________

$\frac{1}{2}$ of $\frac{1}{10}$ = __________

$\frac{5}{12}$ of $\frac{2}{3}$ = __________

$\frac{2}{9}$ of $\frac{4}{7}$ = __________

Answer each question. Write your answer in simplest form.

Mel has a box of donuts, and $\frac{2}{3}$ of the donuts are mini. Out of all the mini donuts, $\frac{3}{4}$ are chocolate. What fraction of the whole box are mini chocolate donuts? ____________

At the Fairview Symphony, $\frac{1}{4}$ of the musicians play string instruments. Of the musicians who play string instruments, $\frac{1}{4}$ play the violin. What fraction of the musicians play the violin? ____________

At her orchard, April estimates that $\frac{5}{8}$ of the apples are red. She also estimates that $\frac{4}{9}$ of the red apples are Gala apples. According to her estimates, what fraction of the apples in her orchard are Gala apples? ____________

At the Atlantic Aquarium, $\frac{5}{6}$ of the animals are fish. On a tour, Jessie learns that $\frac{3}{4}$ of all of the fish at the aquarium are saltwater fish. What fraction of the animals in the aquarium are saltwater fish? ____________

Word problems

Answer each question. Write your answer in simplest form.

Manny, Oliver, and Elena helped paint a mural for their art class. Their art teacher had already done some painting the day before, so there was only $\frac{3}{4}$ of the mural left to paint. Manny painted $\frac{1}{6}$ of the remaining mural, Oliver painted $\frac{1}{2}$ of it, and Elena painted $\frac{1}{3}$ of it.

What fraction of the entire mural did Manny paint? __________

What fraction of the entire mural did Oliver paint? __________

What fraction of the entire mural did Elena paint? __________

Which student painted the greatest fraction of the mural? __________

Let's Learn!

To multiply a mixed number by a fraction, first change the mixed number into an improper fraction. Then multiply across. Try it with $3\frac{1}{2} \times \frac{3}{4}$.
To start, write $3\frac{1}{2}$ as an improper fraction.

$$3\frac{1}{2} = \frac{7}{2}$$

Now, multiply and write your answer as a mixed number.

$$\frac{7}{2} \times \frac{3}{4} = \frac{21}{8} = 2\frac{5}{8}$$

Multiply. Write your answer as a proper fraction or mixed number in simplest form.

$2\frac{3}{4} \times \frac{2}{5} =$ $1\frac{1}{10}$

$\frac{11}{4} \times \frac{2}{5} = \frac{22}{20} = 1\frac{2}{20} = 1\frac{1}{10}$

$\frac{1}{5} \times 1\frac{1}{3} =$ ______

$1\frac{3}{8} \times \frac{2}{3} =$ ______

$2\frac{2}{5} \times \frac{3}{5} =$ ______

$\frac{1}{5} \times 1\frac{3}{4} =$ ______

$5\frac{1}{2} \times \frac{5}{12} =$ ______

$3\frac{2}{3} \times \frac{1}{2} =$ ______

Multiplying mixed numbers

Let's Learn!

You can multiply two mixed numbers the same way. Change both mixed numbers to improper fractions, and then multiply across.

$$1\frac{1}{4} \times 2\frac{1}{3} = \frac{5}{4} \times \frac{7}{3} = \frac{35}{12}$$

$$\frac{35}{12} = 2\frac{11}{12}$$

Multiply. Write your answer as a mixed number in simplest form.

$2\frac{1}{2} \times 1\frac{3}{4} = \underline{4\frac{3}{8}}$

$\frac{5}{2} \times \frac{7}{4} = \frac{35}{8} = 4\frac{3}{8}$

$2\frac{1}{5} \times 1\frac{1}{6} =$ ______

$1\frac{1}{9} \times 1\frac{3}{7} =$ ______

$2\frac{1}{4} \times 4\frac{1}{2} =$ ______

$1\frac{1}{11} \times 3\frac{1}{2} =$ ______

$1\frac{2}{7} \times 1\frac{2}{5} =$ ______

$5\frac{1}{4} \times 1\frac{1}{8} =$ ______

Multiply. Compare each pair of products using >, <, or =.

$1\frac{1}{8} \times 1\frac{3}{4}$ ⓧ $1\frac{2}{5} \times 1\frac{2}{3}$ (circle filled in: $<$)

$\frac{9}{8} \times \frac{7}{4} = \frac{63}{32}$ $\qquad$ $\frac{7}{5} \times \frac{5}{3} = \frac{35}{15}$

$\frac{63}{32} = 1\frac{31}{32}$ $\qquad$ $\frac{35}{15} = 2\frac{1}{3}$

$4\frac{1}{2} \times \frac{1}{12}$ ◯ $3\frac{2}{3} \times \frac{1}{8}$

$1\frac{1}{4} \times \frac{2}{3}$ ◯ $2\frac{1}{3} \times \frac{1}{7}$

$1\frac{3}{4} \times \frac{2}{3}$ ◯ $3\frac{1}{2} \times \frac{1}{3}$

$3\frac{1}{2} \times 1\frac{4}{5}$ ◯ $2\frac{1}{8} \times 2\frac{2}{3}$

$2\frac{1}{10} \times 2\frac{3}{5}$ ◯ $2\frac{1}{2} \times 2\frac{6}{7}$

$3\frac{2}{3} \times 4$ ◯ $3\frac{2}{5} \times 3\frac{3}{4}$

IXL.com
skill ID
6Q4

Multiplying fractions and mixed numbers

Let's review! Multiply. Write your answer as a proper fraction or mixed number in simplest form.

$\frac{5}{8} \times 6 =$ ______

$\frac{2}{9} \times 4 =$ ______

$\frac{2}{7} \times \frac{1}{3} =$ ______

$\frac{7}{12} \times \frac{5}{6} =$ ______

$3\frac{6}{7} \times \frac{3}{10} =$ ______

$\frac{9}{11} \times 1\frac{2}{3} =$ ______

$9 \times 1\frac{3}{10} =$ ______

$1\frac{1}{4} \times 8 =$ ______

$3\frac{4}{7} \times 1\frac{8}{9} =$ ______

$2\frac{1}{8} \times 2\frac{2}{3} =$ ______

Answer each question. Write your answer as a proper fraction or mixed number in simplest form.

Theo needs $1\frac{2}{3}$ cups of flour for each batch of cupcakes he bakes. How many cups of flour will he need for 4 batches of cupcakes? ______

Gia ran around the pond at the park $2\frac{1}{2}$ times. Each lap was $\frac{5}{8}$ of a mile. How many miles did Gia run in total? ______

Jessica worked 5 different days this week, and she worked $1\frac{1}{2}$ hours each day. What is the total number of hours Jessica worked this week? ______

A farmer uses $4\frac{1}{2}$ acres to grow corn. He uses $2\frac{1}{2}$ times as many acres to grow watermelon. How many acres does he use to grow watermelon? ______

Michael used vinegar for a few science experiments. He used $3\frac{3}{4}$ cups of vinegar for his first experiment. Then, he used $\frac{1}{3}$ as much vinegar for his second experiment. How much vinegar did he use for the second experiment? ______

IXL.com
skill ID
5W6

MULTIPLICATION AS SCALING

When you multiply, the answer is often bigger than the number you started with. But not always! See for yourself. Solve each problem below. Then say whether the product is **greater than, less than**, or **equal to** the first number.

$3 \times 1\frac{1}{2} = 4\frac{1}{2}$ The product is GREATER THAN 3.

$3 \times \frac{3}{5} =$ ______ The product is ______ 3.

$3 \times 1 =$ ______ The product is ______ 3.

Go back and look at the second factor in each problem. Is that second factor greater than, less than, or equal to 1? Can you come up with a rule to predict the size of the product?

TRY IT FOR YOURSELF!

Without doing the math, decide whether the product will be greater than or less than the first factor.

$8 \times \frac{1}{2}$ will be LESS than 8.

$\frac{1}{3} \times 3\frac{3}{4}$ will be ______ than $\frac{1}{3}$.

$2 \times 1\frac{5}{12}$ will be ______ than 2.

$\frac{7}{8} \times \frac{8}{9}$ will be ______ than $\frac{7}{8}$.

USING SCALING TO COMPARE

You can also use this idea to compare two products. Can you tell which will have the larger answer, $5 \times \frac{4}{9}$ or $5 \times 1\frac{1}{2}$?

You know that $5 \times \frac{4}{9}$ will be smaller than 5, and $5 \times 1\frac{1}{2}$ will be larger than 5. So, $5 \times 1\frac{1}{2}$ will have the larger answer!

TRY IT FOR YOURSELF!

Without doing the math, compare each pair of products using > or <.

$12 \times \frac{1}{9}$ ◯ $12 \times 1\frac{1}{9}$

$\frac{8}{15} \times 2\frac{1}{5}$ ◯ $\frac{8}{15} \times \frac{1}{5}$

$156 \times 4\frac{1}{7}$ ◯ $156 \times \frac{4}{7}$

$8 \times \frac{6}{7}$ ◯ $8 \times 1\frac{1}{8}$

You can use what you know about scaling to compare other products, too. Keep going! Compare each pair of products using > or <.

$22 \times \frac{1}{6}$ ◯ $32 \times \frac{1}{6}$

$94 \times 1\frac{1}{4}$ ◯ $90 \times \frac{2}{3}$

$16 \times 1\frac{1}{8}$ ◯ $15 \times \frac{7}{8}$

Use the rule to fill in the missing numbers. Write all numbers as proper fractions or mixed numbers in simplest form.

Rule					
Rule: multiply by $\frac{1}{4}$	$\frac{1}{2}$	$\frac{1}{8}$	$\frac{1}{32}$	$\frac{1}{128}$	$\frac{1}{512}$
Rule: multiply by 2	$\frac{2}{3}$			$5\frac{1}{3}$	
Rule: multiply by $\frac{1}{2}$	$\frac{2}{5}$	$\frac{1}{5}$		$\frac{1}{20}$	
Rule: multiply by $1\frac{1}{3}$	$\frac{1}{6}$		$\frac{8}{27}$		
Rule: multiply by 4	$\frac{1}{12}$		$1\frac{1}{3}$		
Rule: multiply by $2\frac{1}{2}$	$\frac{1}{3}$	$\frac{5}{6}$			

IXL.com
skill ID
F66

Let's Learn!

You can divide a whole number by a fraction using a model. Try it with $3 \div \frac{1}{6}$. Start by breaking 3 wholes into $\frac{1}{6}$ pieces.

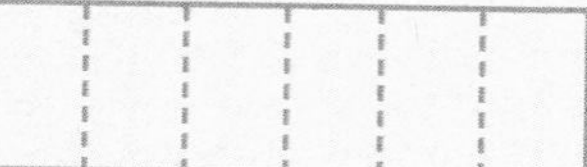
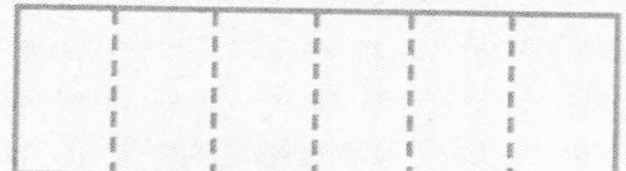

Then, count the number of $\frac{1}{6}$ pieces. There are 18 pieces, so $3 \div \frac{1}{6} = 18$.

Divide. Use the models to help.

$4 \div \frac{1}{2} =$ 8

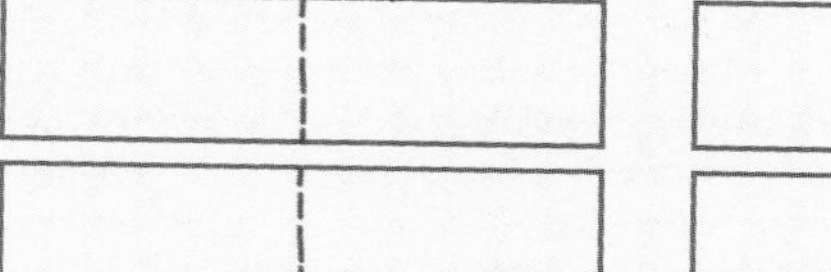
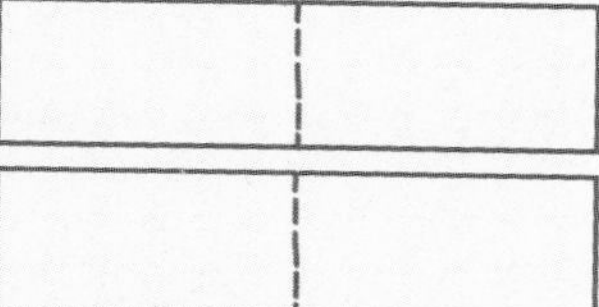

$2 \div \frac{1}{4} =$ ______

$4 \div \frac{1}{3} =$ ______

$2 \div \frac{1}{6} =$ ______

IXL.com skill ID **VDU**

Dividing whole numbers and fractions

Let's Learn!

You can also divide a fraction by a whole number. Try it with $\frac{1}{3} \div 2$. Start with a model of $\frac{1}{3}$. Then divide the $\frac{1}{3}$ piece into 2 pieces. What fraction of the whole is each new piece?

Each new piece is $\frac{1}{6}$ of the whole, so $\frac{1}{3} \div 2 = \frac{1}{6}$.

Divide. Use the models to help.

$\frac{1}{2} \div 4 =$ $\frac{1}{8}$

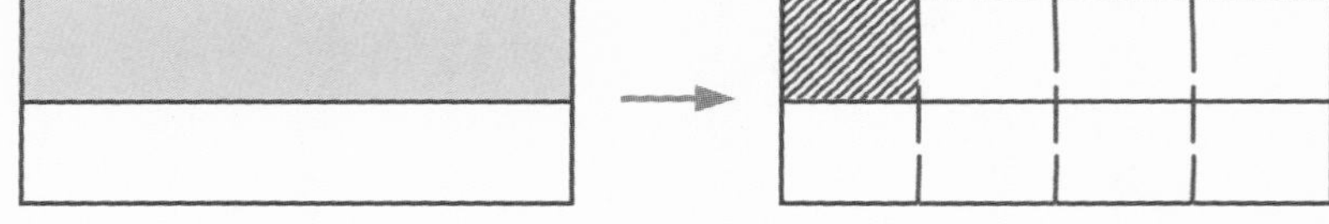

$\frac{1}{5} \div 3 =$ ______

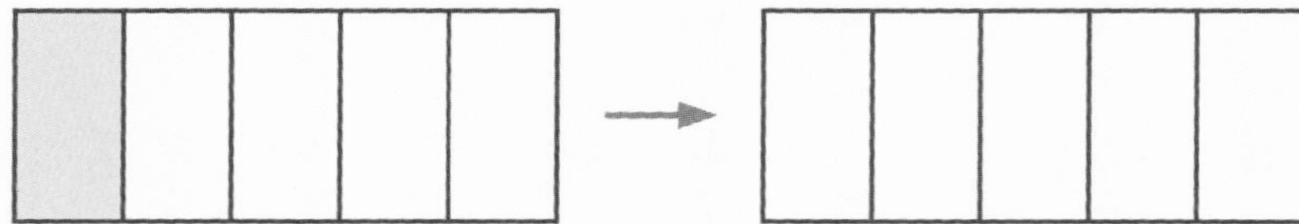

$\frac{1}{3} \div 4 =$ ______

$\frac{1}{4} \div 2 =$ ______

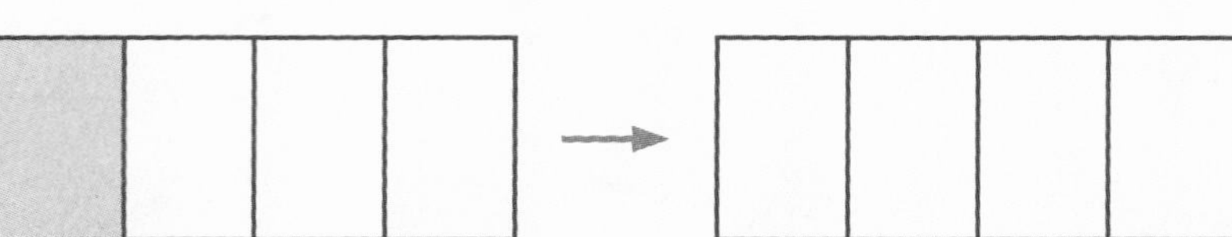

Dividing whole numbers and fractions

Divide. Draw models to help.

$\frac{1}{2} \div 3 =$ $\frac{1}{6}$

$2 \div \frac{1}{3} =$ 6

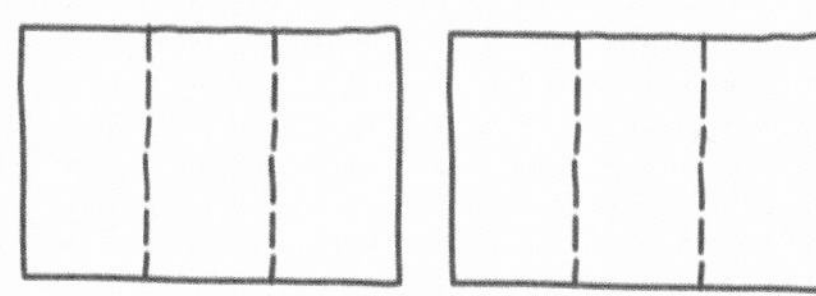

$\frac{1}{5} \div 2 =$ ______

$5 \div \frac{1}{2} =$ ______

$\frac{1}{3} \div 5 =$ ______

$3 \div \frac{1}{5} =$ ______

$\frac{1}{4} \div 3 =$ ______

$4 \div \frac{1}{3} =$ ______

FIND THE PATTERN! What do you notice about the problems in each row? How do these problems and their answers compare?

IXL.com skill ID **A7W**

70 Reciprocals

Let's Learn!

To divide fractions without using models, you can use a **reciprocal**. You can find the reciprocal of a fraction by switching the numerator and the denominator. For example, the reciprocal of $\frac{2}{3}$ is $\frac{3}{2}$.

$$\frac{2}{3} \rightarrow \frac{3}{2}$$

You can find the reciprocal of a whole number, too! First, write the number as a fraction by placing it over 1. Then switch the numerator and the denominator. So, the reciprocal of 4 is $\frac{1}{4}$.

$$4 = \frac{4}{1} \rightarrow \frac{1}{4}$$

Find the reciprocal.

$\frac{2}{7} \rightarrow$ $\frac{7}{2}$

$\frac{9}{11} \rightarrow$ ______

$8 \rightarrow$ ______

$\frac{1}{2} \rightarrow$ ______

$\frac{5}{6} \rightarrow$ ______

$\frac{2}{9} \rightarrow$ ______

$5 \rightarrow$ ______

$\frac{4}{5} \rightarrow$ ______

$\frac{7}{12} \rightarrow$ ______

IXL.com skill ID T9G

$\frac{6}{7} \rightarrow$ ______

$2 \rightarrow$ ______

Let's Learn!

Dividing by a fraction is the same as multiplying by its reciprocal! Try it with $2 \div \frac{1}{5}$. Rewrite the division problem using multiplication. Write the fraction $\frac{1}{5}$ as its reciprocal, $\frac{5}{1}$. Multiply across, and simplify!

$$2 \div \frac{1}{5} \longrightarrow 2 \times \frac{5}{1} = \frac{10}{1} = 10$$

Divide. Write your answer as a proper fraction or mixed number in simplest form.

$\frac{5}{7} \div 3 =$ $\frac{5}{7} \times \frac{1}{3} = \frac{5}{21}$

$\frac{1}{2} \div 2 =$ ______________

$7 \div \frac{2}{3} =$ ______________

$\frac{2}{5} \div 4 =$ ______________

$\frac{4}{5} \div 3 =$ ______________

$\frac{1}{4} \div 8 =$ ______________

$9 \div \frac{7}{10} =$ ______________

$11 \div \frac{3}{5} =$ ______________

TAKE ANOTHER LOOK!

Go back and try these steps for the problems on pages 67 and 68. The answers should be the same!

IXL.com skill ID **FKT**

Dividing fractions

Let's Learn!

You can divide a fraction by a fraction using the same method. Multiply the first fraction by the reciprocal of the second fraction. Try it with $\frac{1}{5} \div \frac{3}{7}$.

$$\frac{1}{5} \div \frac{3}{7} \longrightarrow \frac{1}{5} \times \frac{7}{3}$$

$$\frac{1}{5} \times \frac{7}{3} = \frac{7}{15}$$

Divide. Write your answer as a proper fraction or mixed number in simplest form.

$\frac{1}{3} \div \frac{2}{9} =$ $\frac{1}{3} \times \frac{9}{2} = 1\frac{1}{2}$

$\frac{1}{9} \div \frac{1}{4} =$ __________

$\frac{2}{3} \div \frac{8}{9} =$ __________

$\frac{1}{9} \div \frac{4}{5} =$ __________

$\frac{1}{3} \div \frac{9}{11} =$ __________

$\frac{3}{5} \div \frac{1}{4} =$ __________

$\frac{5}{7} \div \frac{3}{4} =$ __________

$\frac{10}{11} \div \frac{1}{5} =$ __________

$\frac{5}{6} \div \frac{2}{9} =$ __________

$\frac{1}{3} \div \frac{5}{12} =$ __________

Divide. Write your answer as a proper fraction or mixed number in simplest form.

$\frac{2}{5} \div \frac{3}{11} =$ ______

$\frac{1}{8} \div \frac{3}{5} =$ ______

$\frac{9}{10} \div \frac{1}{2} =$ ______

$\frac{5}{12} \div \frac{1}{7} =$ ______

$\frac{2}{9} \div \frac{5}{9} =$ ______

$\frac{3}{7} \div \frac{2}{3} =$ ______

$\frac{1}{5} \div \frac{4}{9} =$ ______

$\frac{7}{11} \div \frac{2}{3} =$ ______

$\frac{1}{6} \div \frac{1}{9} =$ ______

$\frac{6}{7} \div \frac{1}{6} =$ ______

$\frac{9}{10} \div \frac{1}{10} =$ ______

$\frac{7}{12} \div \frac{1}{6} =$ ______

For more practice, visit IXL.com or the IXL mobile app and enter this code in the search bar.

IXL.com skill ID **GL6**

Dividing fractions

Divide. Draw a line to the correct answer in simplest form.

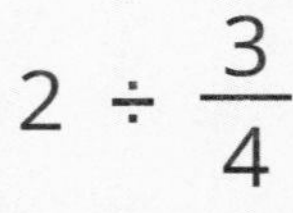

$2 \div \frac{3}{4}$	21
$\frac{5}{7} \div \frac{1}{9}$	$3\frac{1}{5}$
$\frac{1}{2} \div \frac{4}{7}$	$2\frac{2}{3}$
$\frac{9}{10} \div 4$	$\frac{7}{8}$
$3 \div \frac{1}{7}$	$6\frac{3}{7}$
$\frac{4}{5} \div \frac{1}{4}$	$\frac{9}{40}$

Divide. Compare each pair using >, <, or =.

$6 \div \frac{2}{3}$ (>) $4 \div \frac{1}{2}$

$6 \times \frac{3}{2} = \frac{18}{2}$ $\quad$ $4 \times \frac{2}{1} = \frac{8}{1}$

$\frac{18}{2} = 9$ $\quad$ $\frac{8}{1} = 8$

$\frac{1}{6} \div \frac{4}{5}$ ◯ $\frac{1}{8} \div \frac{3}{5}$

$\frac{1}{12} \div \frac{1}{8}$ ◯ $\frac{5}{6} \div \frac{2}{3}$

$\frac{5}{6} \div \frac{1}{9}$ ◯ $\frac{3}{4} \div \frac{1}{7}$

$10 \div \frac{2}{3}$ ◯ $5 \div \frac{1}{3}$

$\frac{3}{11} \div \frac{1}{2}$ ◯ $\frac{7}{11} \div \frac{1}{6}$

Word problems

Answer each question. Write your answer in simplest form.

The owner of an ice cream shop divided $\frac{3}{4}$ of a gallon of sorbet evenly into 12 small containers. How many gallons of sorbet did he put in each container? ________________

Sabrina shared $\frac{6}{7}$ of a bag of dog treats equally among 3 dogs. What fraction of the bag did each dog get? ________________

The chef at Rosa's Italian Kitchen has 7 boxes of pasta. Each serving of pasta is $\frac{1}{8}$ of a box. How many servings of pasta can the chef make? ________________

Jason has $\frac{3}{5}$ of a jar of peanut butter left. He uses $\frac{1}{10}$ of a jar for breakfast each day. How many more days will the jar last? ________________

IXL.com
skill ID
G2N

Let's Learn!

When you divide two whole numbers, you might get a fraction as your answer! For example, if you divide 12 by 16, you get $\frac{12}{16}$ or $\frac{3}{4}$.

$$12 \div 16 = \frac{12}{16} = \frac{3}{4}$$

Divide. Write your answer as a proper fraction or mixed number in simplest form.

$10 \div 7 =$ $\frac{10}{7} = 1\frac{3}{7}$

$8 \div 18 =$ ________

$15 \div 25 =$ ________

$24 \div 10 =$ ________

$35 \div 20 =$ ________

$36 \div 42 =$ ________

$5 \div 60 =$ ________

$48 \div 22 =$ ________

$16 \div 36 =$ ________

$72 \div 11 =$ ________

$9 \div 75 =$ ________

$80 \div 15 =$ ________

78 Word problems

Answer each question. Write your answer as a proper fraction or mixed number in simplest form.

A camp counselor bought 8 quarts of chocolate milk for his 6 campers to share. How much chocolate milk is there for each camper? ____________

Lilly splits a 3-ounce bag of raisins into 4 different containers to make trail mix. How many ounces of raisins are in each container? ____________

Mrs. Aimes brought 2 pounds of her famous macaroni and cheese to a cookout. After 12 people went through the line, the whole dish was gone! If all 12 people got about the same amount, how many pounds of macaroni and cheese did each person eat? ____________

Terry made a 4-layer red velvet cake. He split 15 cups of cake batter into 4 cake pans. How many cups of batter were in each pan? ____________

Jennifer ran 4 miles in 34 minutes. If she ran about the same speed the entire time, how long did it take her to run 1 mile? ____________

IXL.com
skill ID
CTD

Solve. Write your answer as a proper fraction or mixed number in simplest form.

$\frac{5}{6} + \frac{1}{4} =$ ________

$4 \div \frac{2}{5} =$ ________

$7 - 1\frac{3}{4} =$ ________

$4\frac{1}{3} + \frac{1}{9} =$ ________

$9 \times \frac{5}{6} =$ ________

$\frac{3}{4} \div \frac{2}{3} =$ ________

$2\frac{7}{9} + 1\frac{2}{3} =$ ________

$12 \times \frac{8}{9} =$ ________

$\frac{5}{8} - \frac{1}{7} =$ ________

$\frac{1}{9} \div \frac{5}{6} =$ ________

$\frac{1}{2} \times \frac{5}{7} =$ ________

$10\frac{5}{12} - 5\frac{1}{6} =$ ________

IXL.com skill ID **VFX**

Follow the path from start to finish. Write your answers as proper fractions or mixed numbers in simplest form.

START

$\frac{1}{2}$ → $\times \frac{1}{2}$ → □

↓ $+ \frac{3}{8}$

□ ← $+ \frac{1}{2}$ ← □

↓ $\times 4$

□ → $- 3\frac{3}{5}$ → □ → $\div \frac{1}{3}$ → □

↑ $+ 4\frac{1}{3}$

↑ $- \frac{1}{6}$

FINISH

Fill in the missing numbers.

$$\frac{1}{2} \times \frac{\square}{3} = \frac{5}{6}$$

$$\frac{\square}{5} + \frac{3}{10} = \frac{1}{2}$$

$$\frac{\square}{6} - \frac{2}{3} = \frac{1}{6}$$

$$\frac{\square}{10} + \frac{2}{5} = 1\frac{1}{10}$$

$$6 \div \frac{\square}{4} = 24$$

$$1\frac{1}{8} - \frac{\square}{4} = \frac{3}{8}$$

$$\frac{1}{3} + \frac{\square}{2} = \frac{5}{6}$$

$$\frac{2}{5} \times \frac{\square}{6} = \frac{1}{3}$$

$$1\frac{3}{4} \times \frac{\square}{8} = \frac{7}{32}$$

$$\frac{1}{7} \div \frac{1}{2} = \frac{\square}{7}$$

Problem solving

Answer each question. Write your answer as a proper fraction or mixed number in simplest form.

I am $\frac{2}{3}$ of 12. What number am I?

If you add $\frac{1}{4}$ to me, you get $\frac{3}{8}$. What number am I?

If you take away $\frac{2}{5}$ from me, you get $\frac{4}{15}$. What number am I?

I am $\frac{6}{7}$ divided by $\frac{3}{4}$. What number am I?

I am $\frac{5}{11}$ of 9. What number am I?

If you take away $1\frac{1}{5}$ from me, you get $4\frac{1}{3}$. What number am I?

Answer each question. Write your answer as a proper fraction or mixed number in simplest form.

A group of 6 friends are in a book club together, and $\frac{2}{3}$ of them have already finished the book. How many of the friends have already finished the book? ________________

Jessica is measuring spices for a recipe. She uses $1\frac{1}{4}$ teaspoons of cinnamon, $\frac{1}{2}$ of a teaspoon of nutmeg, and $\frac{3}{4}$ of a teaspoon of pepper. How many teaspoons of spices does she use altogether? ________________

Irene is picking plums from the trees in her family's backyard. She puts the plums into boxes that can hold $4\frac{1}{2}$ pounds each. If she fills $2\frac{3}{4}$ of the boxes, how many pounds of plums has she picked? ________________

Angie used a scale to separate $\frac{5}{6}$ of a pound of clay into 2 equally-sized pieces for her and her brother. Her brother took his piece and added $\frac{3}{4}$ of a pound of clay to it. How many pounds is her brother's piece of clay? ________________

Answer each question. Write your answer as a proper fraction or mixed number in simplest form.

Vivian owns a doggy day care. Each dog has a specific amount of food it should eat over the course of a day. Vivian made a chart to keep track of how much food the dogs should eat.

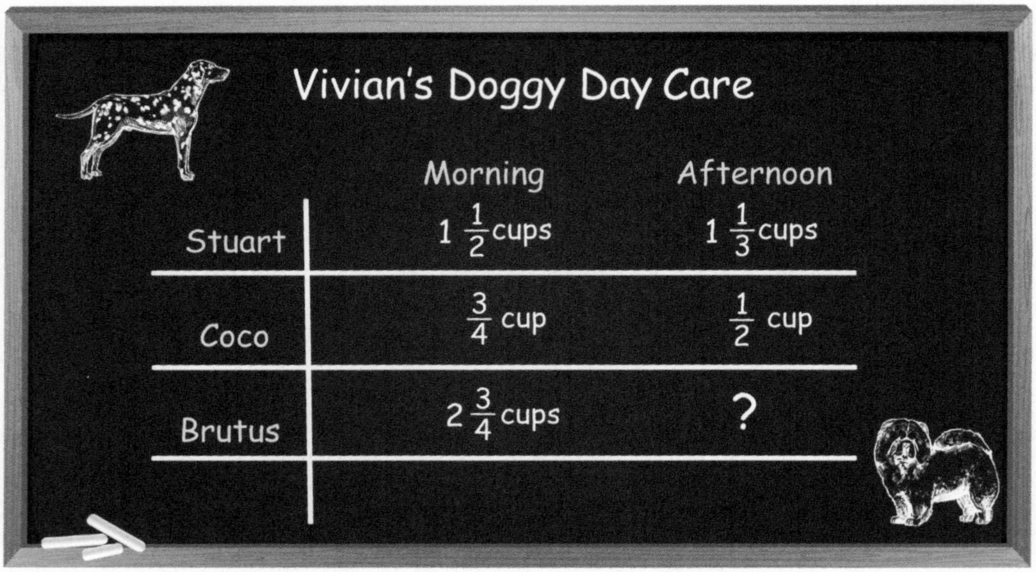

Vivian's Doggy Day Care

	Morning	Afternoon
Stuart	$1\frac{1}{2}$ cups	$1\frac{1}{3}$ cups
Coco	$\frac{3}{4}$ cup	$\frac{1}{2}$ cup
Brutus	$2\frac{3}{4}$ cups	?

How much food should Stuart eat over the course of a day? ____________

Vivian forgot to write down the amount of food Brutus should eat in the afternoon, but she knows he needs to eat a total of $4\frac{1}{12}$ cups. What amount of food should Vivian write down? ____________

Vivian has to feed 5 French bulldogs in the afternoon. She knows they each get the same amount of food as Coco's afternoon meal. How much food does Vivian need in order to feed all 5 French bulldogs this afternoon? ____________

On Tuesday, Coco got to day care late and didn't eat her morning meal. Vivian decided to share her meal between 2 puppies. How much food did each puppy get? ____________

Find the perimeter of each shape. Write your answer as a proper fraction or mixed number in simplest form.

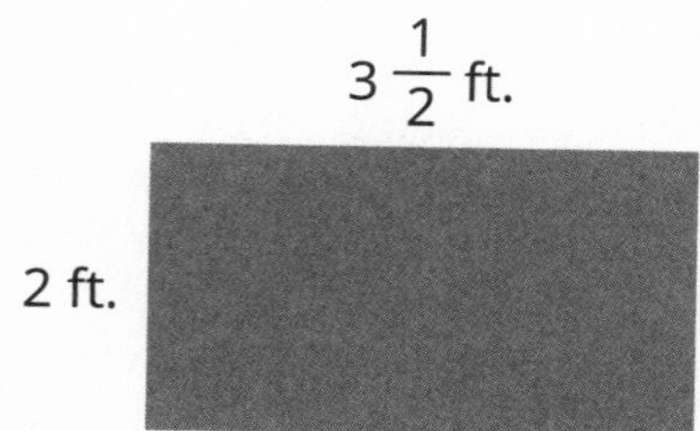

Perimeter = 11 FT.

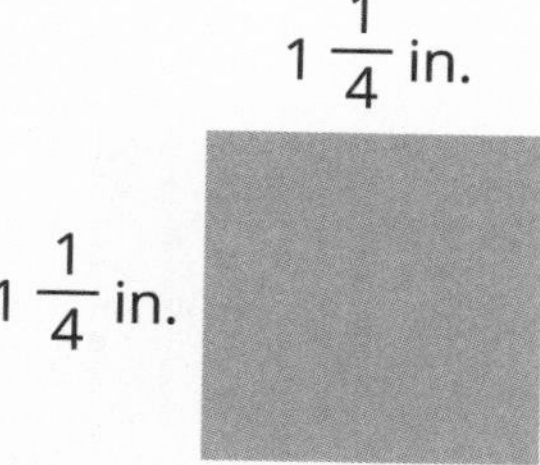

Perimeter = ______________

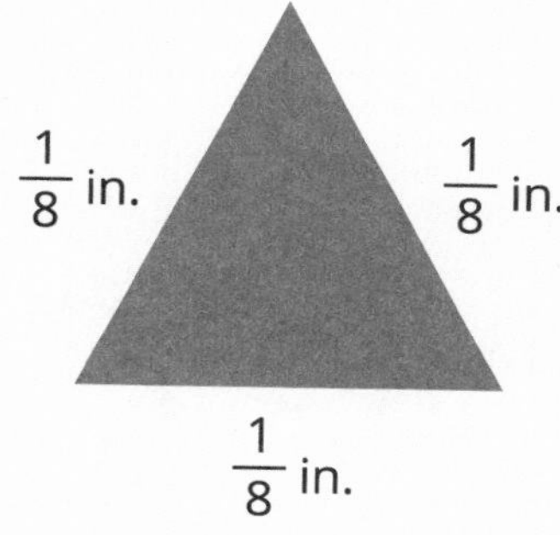

Perimeter = ______________

Perimeter = ______________

$5\frac{1}{2}$ ft. $5\frac{1}{2}$ ft.

$5\frac{1}{4}$ ft.

Perimeter = ______________

Write each missing side length as a proper fraction or mixed number in simplest form.

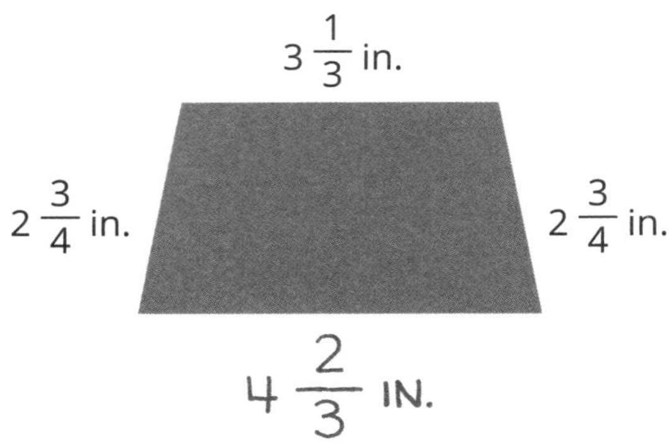

Perimeter = $13\frac{1}{2}$ in.

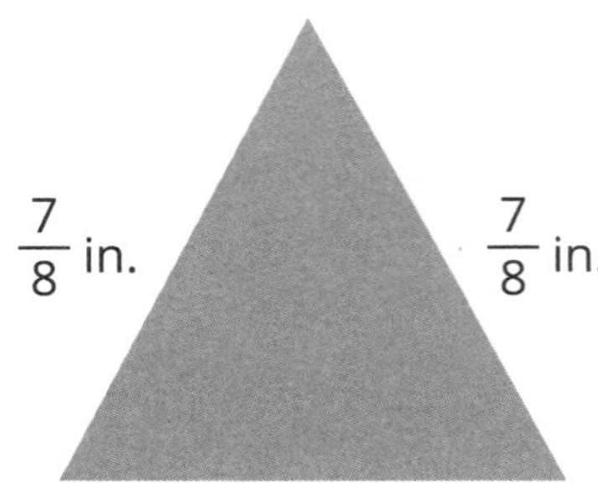

Perimeter = $2\frac{1}{2}$ in.

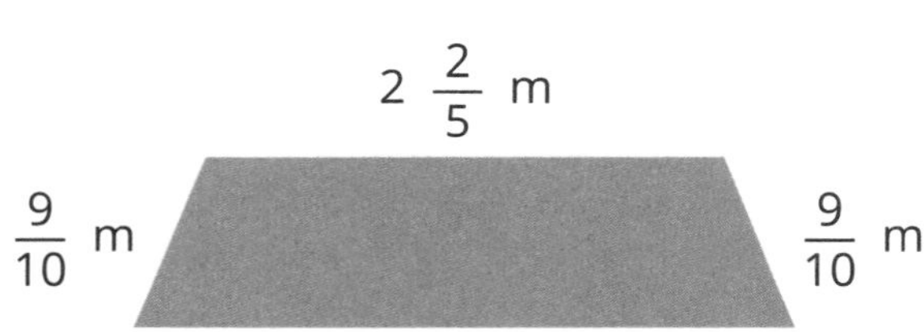

Perimeter = $7\frac{7}{10}$ m

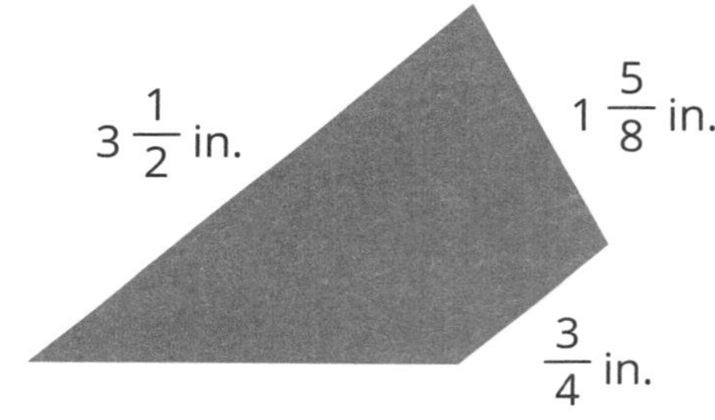

Perimeter = $8\frac{5}{8}$ in.

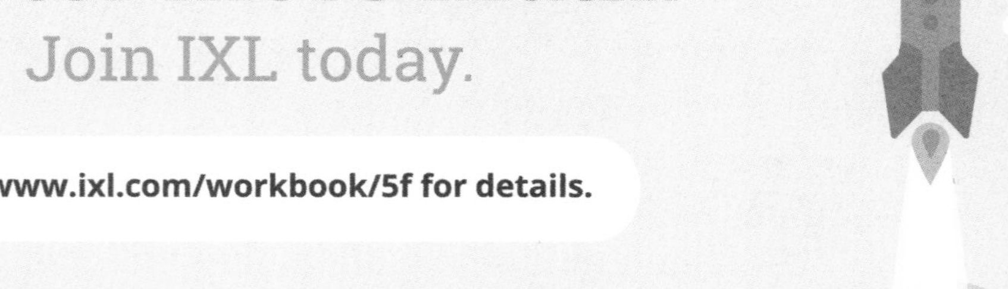
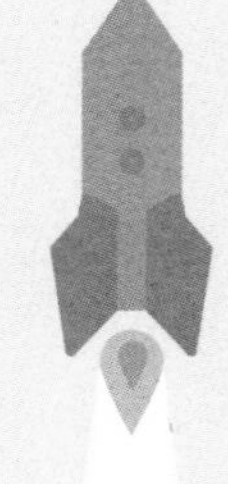

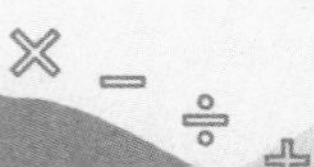

Find the area of each shape. Write your answer as a proper fraction or mixed number in simplest form.

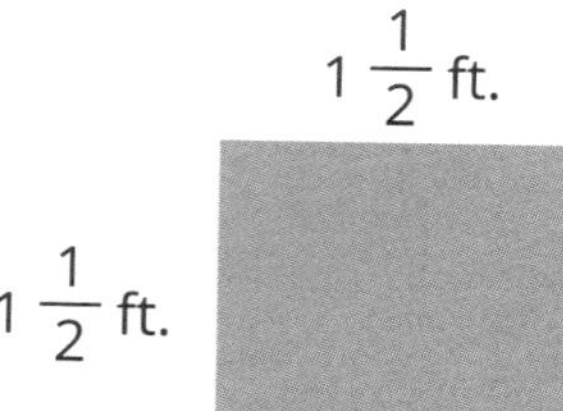

Area = $2\frac{1}{4}$ FT.^{2}

$\frac{2}{5}$ m

$\frac{1}{10}$ m

Area = ______________

2 in.

$\frac{1}{8}$ in.

Area = ______________

$2\frac{1}{4}$ ft.

$2\frac{1}{4}$ ft.

Area = ______________

$4\frac{1}{2}$ cm

$1\frac{3}{5}$ cm

Area = ______________

$3\frac{1}{2}$ in.

$1\frac{1}{8}$ in.

Area = ______________

IXL.com
skill ID
PMV

Area of compound shapes

Find the area of each shape. Write your answer as a proper fraction or mixed number in simplest form.

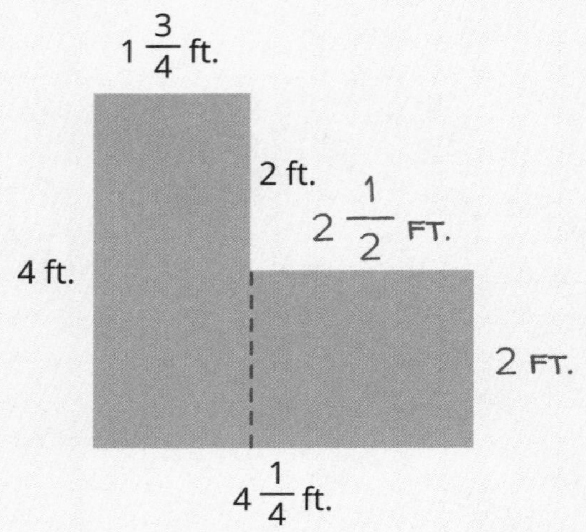

Area = 12 FT.^{2}

$4 - 2 = 2$ FT.

$4\frac{1}{4} - 1\frac{3}{4} = 2\frac{1}{2}$ FT.

$2\frac{1}{2} \times 2 = 5$ $4 \times 1\frac{3}{4} = 7$

$5 + 7 = 12$

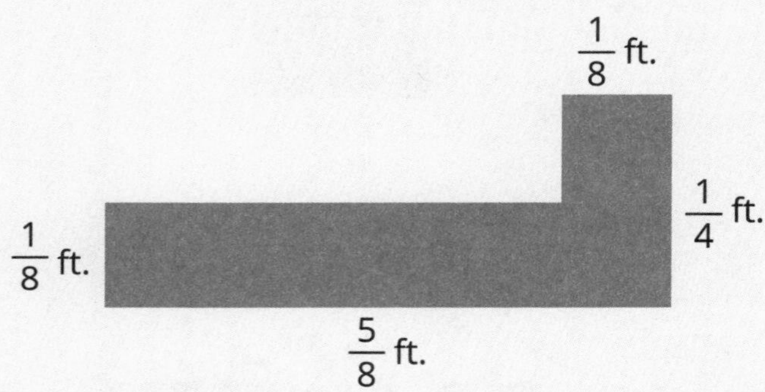

Area = ____________

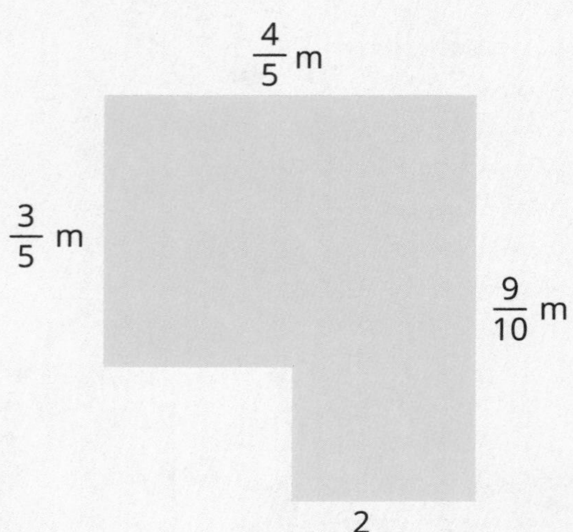

Area = ____________

Answer each question. Write your answer as a proper fraction or mixed number in simplest form.

Leslie's blanket has a length and width of $4\frac{1}{3}$ feet. What is the area of her blanket? ________________

Brittany bought a new TV for her wall. The TV is $1\frac{1}{5}$ meters by $\frac{7}{10}$ meters. How much space will the TV take up on her wall? ________________

The window in Brandon's bedroom has an area of $12\frac{5}{8}$ square feet. The window in his kitchen has a length of $4\frac{1}{2}$ feet and a width of $2\frac{3}{4}$ feet. How much larger is Brandon's bedroom window than his kitchen window? ________________

The bottom of Christopher's aquarium tank has an area of $\frac{3}{5}$ of a square meter. If the bottom of the aquarium has a length of $\frac{3}{4}$ of a meter, what is the width? ________________

Adding and subtracting fractions

Add or subtract. Write your answer in simplest form.

$\frac{1}{3} + \frac{1}{3} =$ ______

$\frac{3}{7} + \frac{2}{7} =$ ______

$\frac{11}{12} - \frac{3}{4} =$ ______

$\frac{2}{3} - \frac{1}{6} =$ ______

$\frac{3}{5} + \frac{1}{9} =$ ______

$\frac{7}{9} - \frac{1}{4} =$ ______

$\frac{3}{4} + \frac{2}{5} =$ ______

$\frac{5}{6} + \frac{1}{2} =$ ______

$\frac{9}{10} - \frac{1}{3} =$ ______

$\frac{8}{11} - \frac{1}{4} =$ ______

$\frac{4}{7} + \frac{1}{2} =$ ______

$\frac{7}{12} - \frac{3}{8} =$ ______

IXL.com
skill ID
ZH5

Add or subtract. Write your answer as a mixed number in simplest form.

$2\frac{1}{2} + \frac{1}{3} =$ ______

$4\frac{5}{6} - 2\frac{1}{3} =$ ______

$5\frac{1}{7} - \frac{3}{4} =$ ______

$6\frac{1}{2} + 4\frac{4}{5} =$ ______

$2\frac{1}{2} - 1\frac{1}{8} =$ ______

$7 + 4\frac{1}{12} =$ ______

$4 - 2\frac{7}{9} =$ ______

$6\frac{2}{3} - \frac{1}{2} =$ ______

$1\frac{3}{8} + \frac{1}{5} =$ ______

$7\frac{1}{10} - \frac{4}{5} =$ ______

$9\frac{1}{4} - \frac{6}{7} =$ ______

$1\frac{2}{3} + 4\frac{4}{5} =$ ______

Fill in the missing numbers. Each row, column, and diagonal will add to the same number, called a magic sum. Write all missing numbers as proper fractions or mixed numbers in simplest form.

Magic sum: 5

$2\frac{2}{3}$	$\frac{1}{3}$	2
1	$1\frac{2}{3}$	$2\frac{1}{3}$
$1\frac{1}{3}$	3	$\frac{2}{3}$

Magic sum: $2\frac{1}{2}$

$\frac{2}{3}$	$\frac{1}{2}$	
	$\frac{5}{6}$	

Magic sum: $1\frac{1}{4}$

		$\frac{7}{12}$
	$\frac{3}{4}$	$\frac{1}{6}$

Magic sum: $4\frac{1}{2}$

	$1\frac{1}{2}$	
$1\frac{4}{5}$	$1\frac{3}{10}$	

IXL.com skill ID **XHJ**

Answer each question. Write your answer as a proper fraction or mixed number in simplest form.

Jenna tried to make pancakes for breakfast. Out of all the pancakes she made, $\frac{3}{8}$ were burnt and $\frac{1}{4}$ were undercooked. What fraction of the pancakes were either burnt or undercooked? ________________

In the Franklin Elementary School choir, $\frac{1}{3}$ of the singers are fourth graders and $\frac{1}{2}$ are fifth graders. What fraction of the choir members are in fourth or fifth grade? ________________

Jonah is feeding goats at a petting zoo. He has a 3-pound sack of goat food and hands $1\frac{5}{8}$ pounds to his sister so she can help. How many pounds of goat food does Jonah have left? ________________

Naya made $2\frac{3}{4}$ quarts of ice cream using her new ice cream maker. She gave $\frac{3}{8}$ of a quart to her friend and then made $1\frac{1}{4}$ more quarts. How many quarts of ice cream does Naya have now? ________________

Perimeter

Find the perimeter of each shape. Write your answer as a proper fraction or mixed number in simplest form.

$1\frac{2}{5}$ m

$1\frac{2}{5}$ m

Perimeter = ____________

2 ft.

$\frac{2}{5}$ ft.

Perimeter = ____________

$2\frac{3}{5}$ m

$\frac{9}{10}$ m

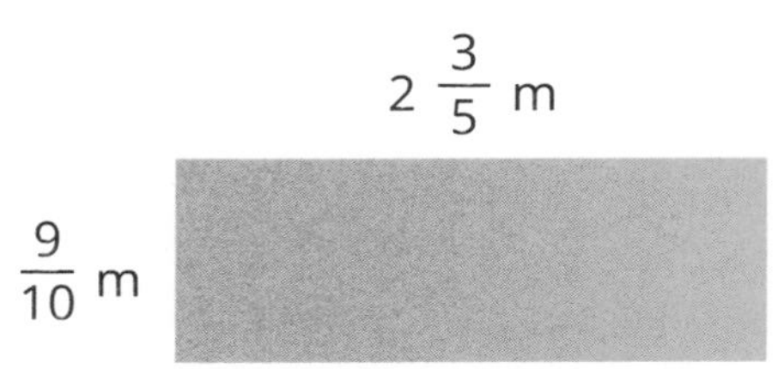

Perimeter = ____________

$5\frac{7}{8}$ in.

$5\frac{7}{8}$ in.

5 in.

Perimeter = ____________

Write each missing side length as a proper fraction or mixed number in simplest form.

$3\frac{1}{8}$ in.

$2\frac{1}{2}$ in.

$2\frac{1}{2}$ in.

Perimeter = $11\frac{3}{4}$ in.

$4\frac{3}{4}$ in.

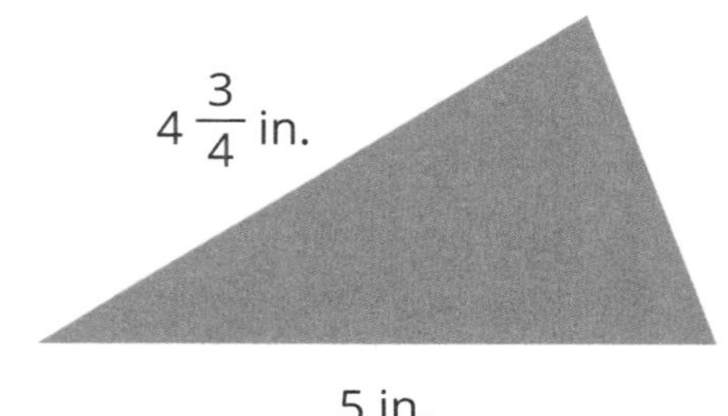

5 in.

Perimeter = $11\frac{7}{8}$ in.

Multiply. Try to be quick! Write your answer as a proper fraction or mixed number in simplest form.

$\frac{5}{6} \times 2 =$ ______

$\frac{4}{5} \times 9 =$ ______

$3 \times \frac{8}{9} =$ ______

$12 \times \frac{5}{12} =$ ______

$\frac{1}{2} \times \frac{1}{3} =$ ______

$\frac{3}{4} \times \frac{2}{7} =$ ______

$\frac{1}{5} \times \frac{3}{8} =$ ______

$\frac{1}{7} \times \frac{3}{10} =$ ______

$\frac{5}{12} \times \frac{1}{6} =$ ______

$\frac{9}{11} \times \frac{1}{2} =$ ______

$\frac{6}{7} \times \frac{1}{9} =$ ______

Multiplying fractions and mixed numbers

Multiply. Write your answer as a proper fraction or mixed number in simplest form.

$\frac{7}{8} \times 2\frac{1}{2} =$ ______

$1\frac{3}{7} \times \frac{2}{3} =$ ______

$3 \times 1\frac{3}{8} =$ ______

$1\frac{1}{3} \times 3\frac{2}{3} =$ ______

$2\frac{1}{2} \times 1\frac{1}{6} =$ ______

$1\frac{1}{10} \times 2\frac{1}{4} =$ ______

$1\frac{1}{9} \times 1\frac{4}{7} =$ ______

$2\frac{3}{5} \times 2\frac{3}{4} =$ ______

$1\frac{1}{7} \times 4\frac{5}{6} =$ ______

$5\frac{8}{9} \times 1\frac{1}{4} =$ ______

Find the area of each shape. Write your answer as a proper fraction or mixed number in simplest form.

$4\frac{1}{4}$ in.

$\frac{1}{4}$ in.

Area = ________________

$6\frac{1}{8}$ in.

2 in.

Area = ________________

3 in.

$\frac{7}{8}$ in.

Area = ________________

$\frac{9}{10}$ m

$\frac{2}{5}$ m

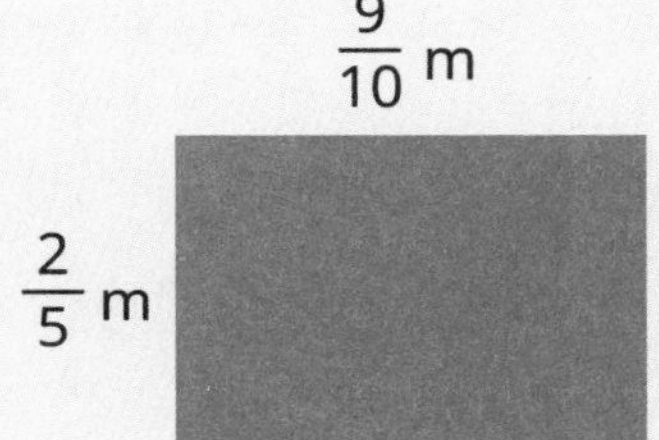

Area = ________________

$2\frac{2}{3}$ in.

$5\frac{1}{4}$ in.

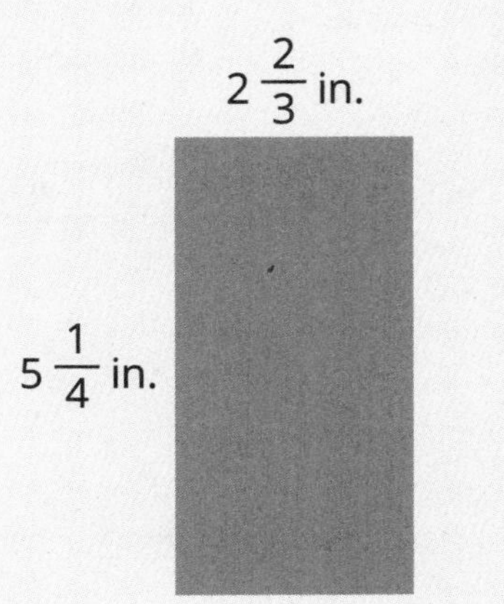

Area = ________________

$1\frac{1}{5}$ m

5 m

Area = ________________

Dividing fractions

Divide. Write your answer as a proper fraction or mixed number in simplest form.

$4 \div \frac{2}{3} =$ ______

$\frac{5}{6} \div 3 =$ ______

$\frac{3}{4} \div \frac{1}{4} =$ ______

$1 \div \frac{1}{5} =$ ______

$\frac{1}{2} \div 6 =$ ______

$\frac{1}{3} \div \frac{4}{9} =$ ______

$12 \div \frac{3}{4} =$ ______

$\frac{3}{8} \div 12 =$ ______

$\frac{2}{3} \div \frac{3}{5} =$ ______

$5 \div \frac{5}{7} =$ ______

$\frac{7}{9} \div 8 =$ ______

$\frac{7}{10} \div \frac{1}{5} =$ ______

IXL.com
skill ID
3L9

Write the missing length or width as a proper fraction or mixed number in simplest form.

$\frac{1}{2}$ in.

$\frac{1}{2}$ in.

Area = $\frac{1}{4}$ in.^{2}

$\frac{1}{2}$ ft.

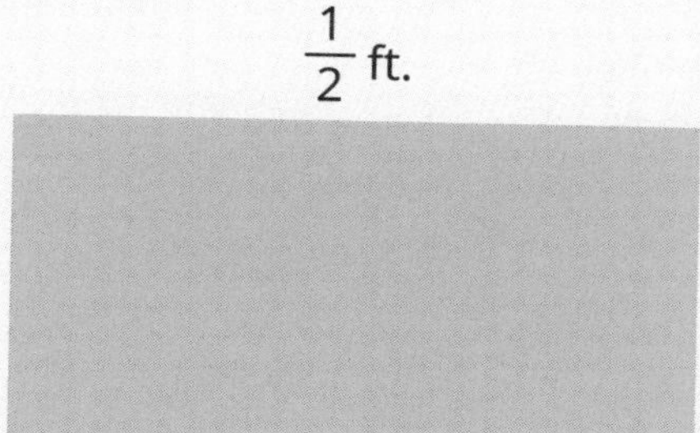

Area = $\frac{1}{8}$ ft.^{2}

2 in.

Area = $\frac{1}{2}$ in.^{2}

$\frac{1}{5}$ m

Area = $\frac{3}{50}$ m^2

Area of compound shapes

Find the area of each shape. Write your answer as a proper fraction or mixed number in simplest form.

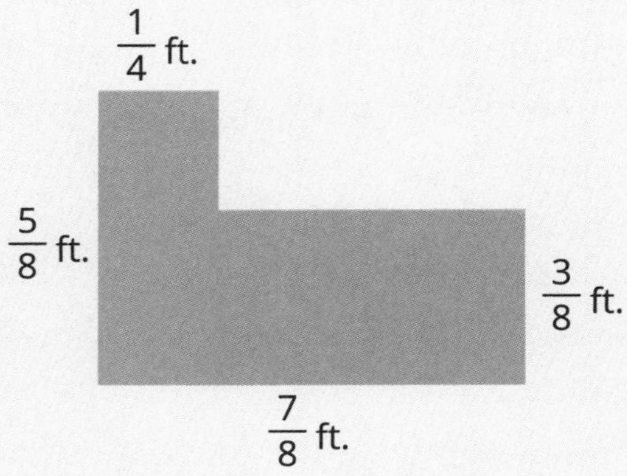

Area = ____________

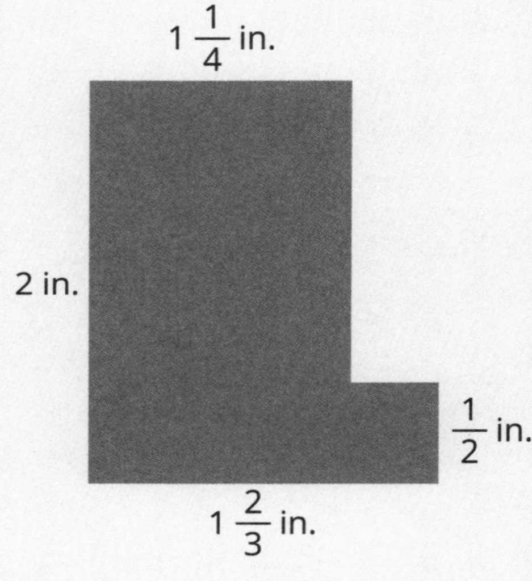

Area = ____________

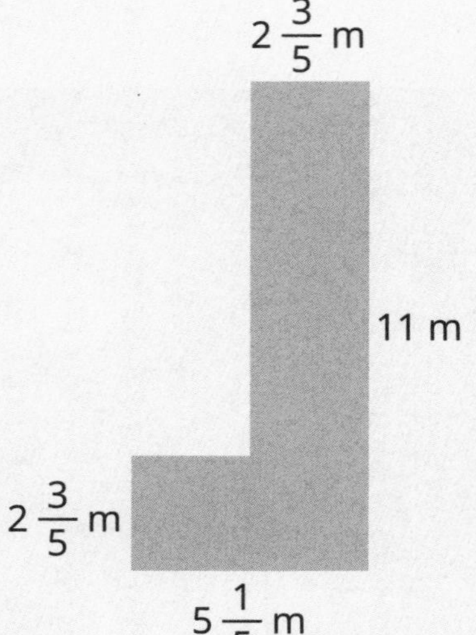

Area = ____________

Answer each question. Write your answer as a proper fraction or mixed number in simplest form.

It takes Adrienne's hockey team $3\frac{1}{2}$ minutes to practice their skating drill. How long would it take to run the drill 5 times? ________________

Aaron is making a few servings of rice to go with a stir-fry. He has 2 cups of rice left in a bag, and he sees that one serving of rice is about $\frac{1}{2}$ of a cup. How many servings of rice can he make? ________________

Sean has $\frac{3}{4}$ of a bag of potting soil. If each of his flower pots uses $\frac{1}{8}$ of a bag of potting soil, how many flower pots can he fill? ________________

Camille wants to make 4 flower arrangements. For each arrangement, she needs $1\frac{1}{2}$ bunches of pink roses and $2\frac{1}{4}$ bunches of red roses. Camille thinks she needs to buy 14 bunches of roses. Is she correct? ________________

Miriam is making her favorite fruit smoothie for breakfast. Use the recipe to answer each question. Write your answer as a proper fraction or mixed number in simplest form.

Fruit Smoothie Recipe

$\frac{1}{4}$ cup frozen strawberries	$\frac{3}{4}$ cup yogurt
$\frac{1}{3}$ cup frozen blueberries	$1\frac{2}{3}$ cups milk

One serving is 3 cups of smoothie

Miriam has 2 cartons of milk in her refrigerator. The first carton has only $\frac{1}{4}$ of a cup of milk, and the second carton is full. If she empties out the first carton, how much milk will she use from the second carton? ________________

She starts by combining the milk and yogurt. How many cups is that in all? ________________

Miriam loves strawberries, so she decides to triple the amount of strawberries in the smoothie. How many cups of strawberries does she use? ________________

She decides to share a serving of the smoothie with her sister. If she splits it equally, how much will they each get?

____

Answer key

Fractions can be written in lots of equivalent ways! On pages that do not ask for simplest form, this answer key includes both the answer your child is most likely to write down and its simplest form. Keep in mind that other answers may also be correct.

PAGE 2

$\frac{1}{4}$ $\quad$ $\frac{2}{6}$ or $\frac{1}{3}$ $\quad$ $\frac{1}{3}$

$\frac{6}{10}$ or $\frac{3}{5}$ $\quad$ $\frac{2}{8}$ or $\frac{1}{4}$ $\quad$ $\frac{3}{4}$

Placement of shading may vary.

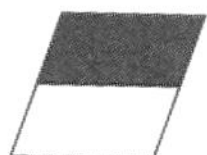 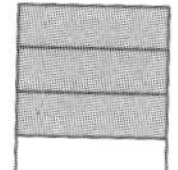 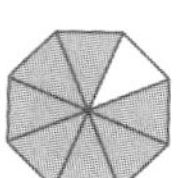

PAGE 3

$\frac{5}{6}$ $\quad$ $\frac{1}{4}$

$\frac{4}{11}$ $\quad$ $\frac{5}{10}$ or $\frac{1}{2}$

Placement of shading may vary.

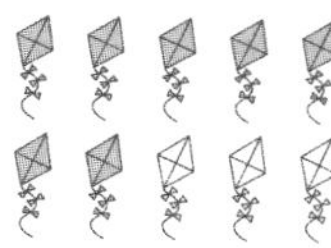

PAGE 4

$\frac{2}{5}$

$\frac{3}{6}$ or $\frac{1}{2}$

$\frac{2}{10}$ or $\frac{1}{5}$

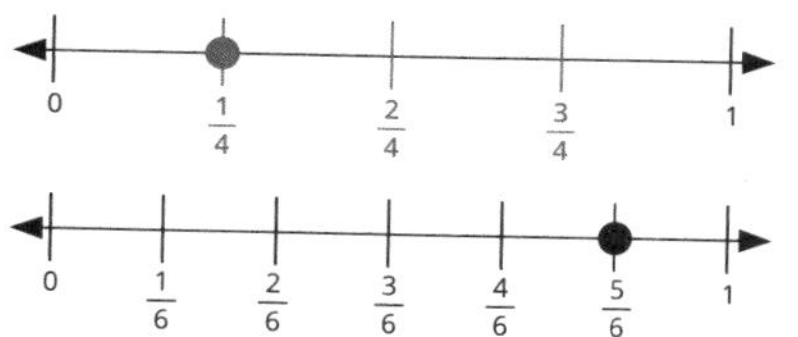

PAGE 4, *continued*

0 $\quad$ $\frac{1}{7}$ $\quad$ $\frac{2}{7}$ $\quad$ $\frac{3}{7}$ $\quad$ $\frac{4}{7}$ $\quad$ $\frac{5}{7}$ $\quad$ $\frac{6}{7}$ $\quad$ 1

PAGE 5

Answers may vary. Some possible answers are shown below.

$\frac{3}{4} = \frac{9}{12}$ $\quad$ $\frac{4}{6} = \frac{2}{3}$

$\frac{5}{9} = \frac{10}{18}$ $\quad$ $\frac{6}{9} = \frac{2}{3}$

$\frac{1}{10} = \frac{2}{20}$ $\quad$ $\frac{2}{11} = \frac{4}{22}$

$\frac{9}{18} = \frac{1}{2}$ $\quad$ $\frac{10}{24} = \frac{5}{12}$

$\frac{15}{25} = \frac{3}{5}$ $\quad$ $\frac{7}{21} = \frac{1}{3}$

Other possible answers are shown below:

$\frac{6}{8}$ $\quad$ $\frac{8}{12}$

$\frac{15}{27}$ $\quad$ $\frac{12}{18}$

$\frac{3}{30}$ $\quad$ $\frac{10}{55}$

$\frac{18}{36}$ $\quad$ $\frac{20}{48}$

$\frac{30}{50}$ $\quad$ $\frac{14}{42}$

PAGE 6

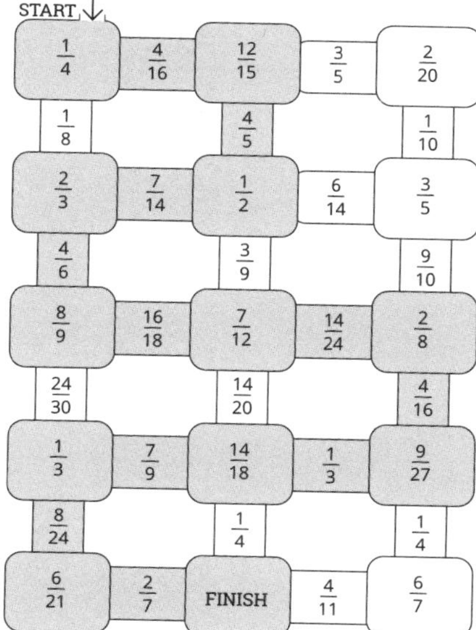

PAGE 7

Factors of 7: 1, (7) $\quad$ $\frac{7}{14} = \frac{1}{2}$

Factors of 14: 1, 2, (7), 14

Factors of 10: 1, 2, (5), 10 $\quad$ $\frac{10}{25} = \frac{2}{5}$

Factors of 25: 1, (5), 25

Factors of 8: 1, (2), 4, 8 $\quad$ $\frac{8}{22} = \frac{4}{11}$

Factors of 22: 1, (2), 11, 22

PAGE 8

$\frac{15}{20} = \frac{3}{4}$ $\quad$ $\frac{6}{10} = \frac{3}{5}$

$\frac{3}{24} = \frac{1}{8}$ $\quad$ $\frac{14}{20} = \frac{7}{10}$

$\frac{5}{25} = \frac{1}{5}$ $\quad$ $\frac{9}{18} = \frac{1}{2}$

$\frac{16}{40} = \frac{2}{5}$ $\quad$ $\frac{20}{48} = \frac{5}{12}$

$\frac{5}{45} = \frac{1}{9}$ $\quad$ $\frac{16}{24} = \frac{2}{3}$

$\frac{32}{36} = \frac{8}{9}$ $\quad$ $\frac{18}{30} = \frac{3}{5}$

$\frac{25}{45} = \frac{5}{9}$ $\quad$ $\frac{30}{36} = \frac{5}{6}$

PAGE 9

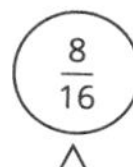

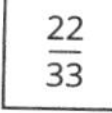

$\frac{6}{8}$ $\quad$ $\frac{12}{18}$ $\quad$ $\frac{27}{36}$ $\quad$ $\frac{9}{12}$

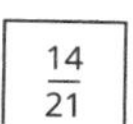

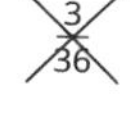

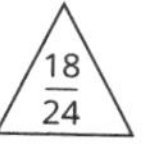

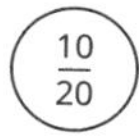

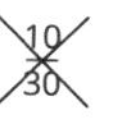

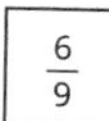

Answer key

PAGE 10

Placement of shading may vary.

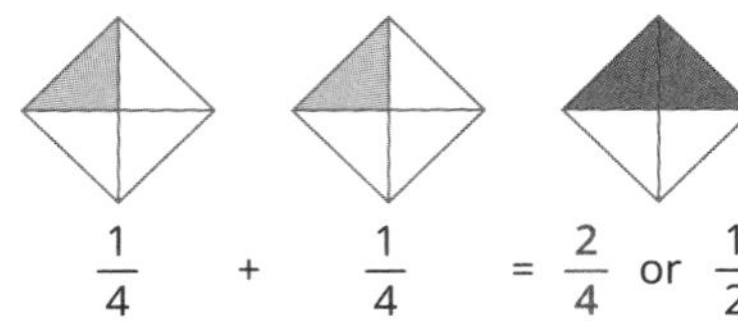

$\frac{1}{4} + \frac{1}{4} = \frac{2}{4}$ or $\frac{1}{2}$

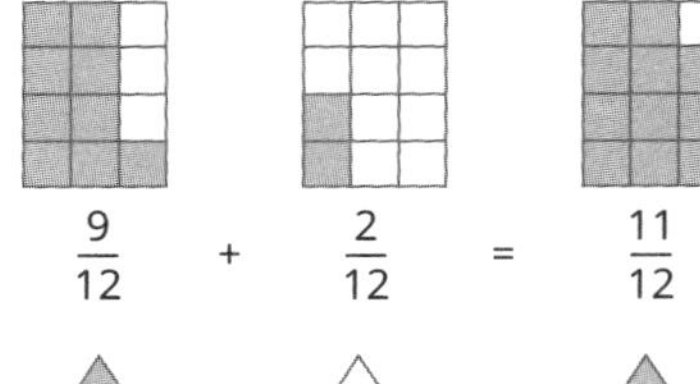

$\frac{9}{12} + \frac{2}{12} = \frac{11}{12}$

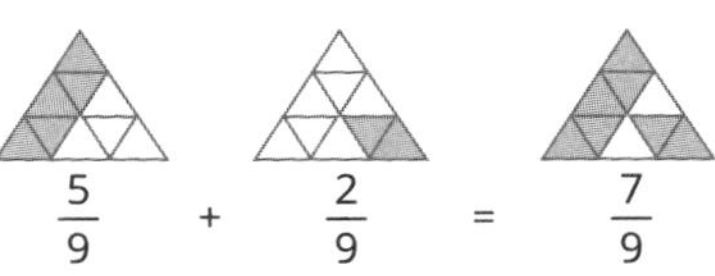

$\frac{5}{9} + \frac{2}{9} = \frac{7}{9}$

PAGE 11

Placement of shading may vary.

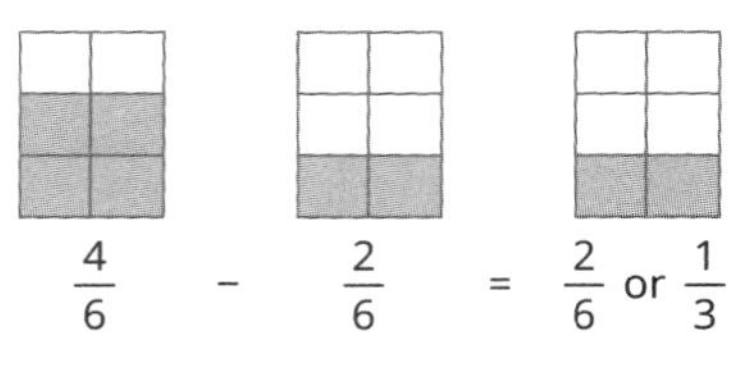

$\frac{4}{6} - \frac{2}{6} = \frac{2}{6}$ or $\frac{1}{3}$

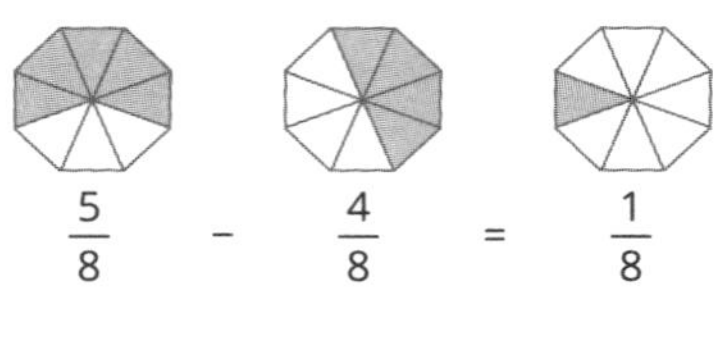

$\frac{5}{8} - \frac{4}{8} = \frac{1}{8}$

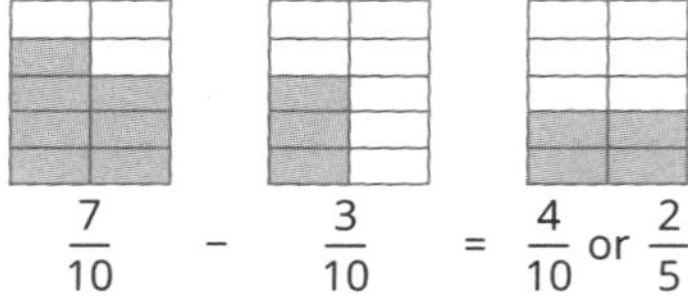

$\frac{7}{10} - \frac{3}{10} = \frac{4}{10}$ or $\frac{2}{5}$

PAGE 12

$\frac{2}{9} + \frac{4}{9} = \frac{2}{3}$

$\frac{4}{7} - \frac{1}{7} = \frac{3}{7}$

$\frac{4}{15} + \frac{8}{15} = \frac{4}{5}$

$\frac{5}{14} + \frac{3}{14} = \frac{4}{7}$

$\frac{1}{33} + \frac{4}{33} = \frac{5}{33}$

$\frac{7}{29} - \frac{5}{29} = \frac{2}{29}$

$\frac{9}{10} - \frac{7}{10} = \frac{1}{5}$

$\frac{1}{8} + \frac{3}{8} = \frac{1}{2}$

$\frac{10}{11} - \frac{2}{11} = \frac{8}{11}$

$\frac{7}{12} - \frac{5}{12} = \frac{1}{6}$

$\frac{27}{50} - \frac{3}{50} = \frac{12}{25}$

$\frac{7}{81} + \frac{2}{81} = \frac{1}{9}$

PAGE 13

$\frac{4}{5} - \frac{1}{5} = \frac{3}{5}$

$\frac{7}{15} + \frac{6}{15} = \frac{13}{15}$

$\frac{1}{6} + \frac{4}{6} = \frac{5}{6}$

$\frac{7}{12} - \frac{4}{12} = \frac{3}{12}$

$\frac{2}{18} + \frac{14}{18} = \frac{16}{18}$

$\frac{12}{14} - \frac{9}{14} = \frac{3}{14}$

$\frac{13}{19} + \frac{4}{19} = \frac{17}{19}$

$\frac{3}{13} + \frac{9}{13} = \frac{12}{13}$

$\frac{9}{10} - \frac{8}{10} = \frac{1}{10}$

$\frac{10}{11} - \frac{4}{11} = \frac{6}{11}$

$\frac{1}{7} + \frac{5}{7} = \frac{6}{7}$

$\frac{11}{17} - \frac{6}{17} = \frac{5}{17}$

$\frac{7}{20} + \frac{8}{20} = \frac{15}{20}$

PAGE 14

Placement of shading may vary.

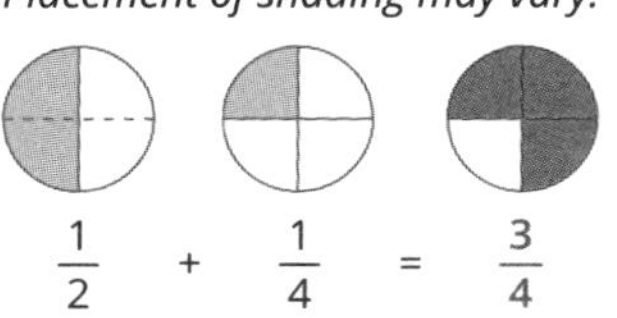

$\frac{1}{2} + \frac{1}{4} = \frac{3}{4}$

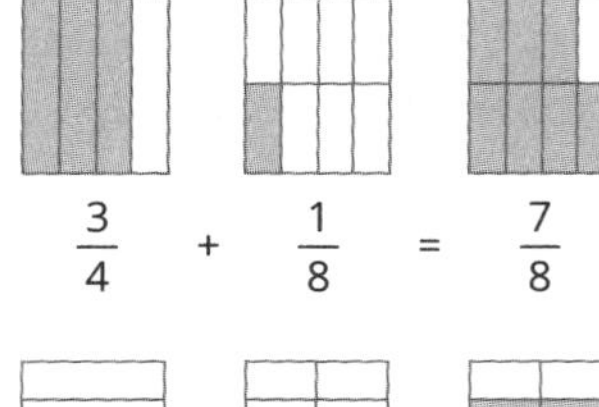

$\frac{3}{4} + \frac{1}{8} = \frac{7}{8}$

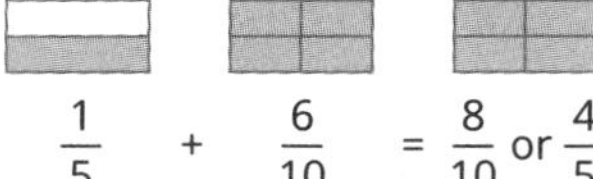

$\frac{1}{5} + \frac{6}{10} = \frac{8}{10}$ or $\frac{4}{5}$

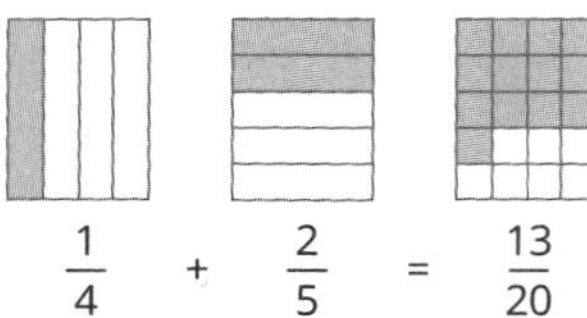

$\frac{1}{4} + \frac{2}{5} = \frac{13}{20}$

PAGE 15

$\frac{1}{4} + \frac{1}{6} = \frac{5}{12}$

$\downarrow \quad \downarrow$

$\frac{3}{12} + \frac{2}{12}$

$\frac{1}{5} + \frac{3}{10} = \frac{1}{2}$

$\downarrow \quad \downarrow$

$\frac{2}{10} + \frac{3}{10}$

PAGE 15, *continued*

$\frac{1}{2} + \frac{4}{9} = \frac{17}{18}$

$\downarrow \quad \downarrow$

$\frac{9}{18} + \frac{8}{18}$

$\frac{1}{4} + \frac{2}{3} = \frac{11}{12}$

$\downarrow \quad \downarrow$

$\frac{3}{12} + \frac{8}{12}$

PAGE 16

$\frac{1}{8} + \frac{3}{4} = \frac{7}{8}$

$\frac{1}{15} + \frac{2}{5} = \frac{7}{15}$

$\frac{3}{8} + \frac{1}{3} = \frac{17}{24}$

$\frac{1}{6} + \frac{2}{3} = \frac{5}{6}$

$\frac{7}{18} + \frac{1}{6} = \frac{5}{9}$

$\frac{1}{7} + \frac{1}{14} = \frac{3}{14}$

$\frac{7}{12} + \frac{1}{4} = \frac{5}{6}$

$\frac{1}{5} + \frac{1}{3} = \frac{8}{15}$

$\frac{1}{2} + \frac{2}{9} = \frac{13}{18}$

$\frac{3}{4} + \frac{1}{16} = \frac{13}{16}$

$\frac{1}{3} + \frac{1}{3} + \frac{1}{12} = \frac{3}{4}$

$\frac{1}{2} + \frac{3}{14} + \frac{1}{7} = \frac{6}{7}$

PAGE 17

$\frac{5}{6}$

$\frac{11}{14}$

$\frac{17}{21}$

$\frac{11}{12}$

PAGE 18

$\frac{1}{2} - \frac{1}{3} = \frac{1}{6}$

$\frac{11}{12} - \frac{5}{6} = \frac{1}{12}$

$\frac{4}{5} - \frac{1}{2} = \frac{3}{10}$

$\frac{3}{10} - \frac{1}{5} = \frac{1}{10}$

$\frac{3}{4} - \frac{1}{3} = \frac{5}{12}$

$\frac{5}{9} - \frac{1}{3} = \frac{2}{9}$

$\frac{7}{8} - \frac{1}{2} = \frac{3}{8}$

$\frac{5}{12} - \frac{1}{4} = \frac{1}{6}$

$\frac{5}{7} - \frac{2}{3} = \frac{1}{21}$

$\frac{3}{11} - \frac{1}{5} = \frac{4}{55}$

PAGE 19

$\frac{2}{3} - \frac{1}{5} = \frac{7}{15}$

$\frac{13}{18} - \frac{1}{2} = \frac{2}{9}$

$\frac{7}{8} - \frac{1}{3} = \frac{13}{24}$

$\frac{11}{14} - \frac{3}{7} = \frac{5}{14}$

PAGE 19, *continued*

$\frac{1}{4} - \frac{1}{9} = \frac{5}{36}$ $\quad$ $\frac{11}{12} - \frac{2}{5} = \frac{31}{60}$

$\frac{9}{10} - \frac{2}{5} = \frac{1}{2}$ $\quad$ $\frac{1}{2} - \frac{4}{9} = \frac{1}{18}$

$\frac{2}{9} - \frac{1}{6} = \frac{1}{18}$ $\quad$ $\frac{5}{6} - \frac{1}{11} = \frac{49}{66}$

$\frac{11}{14} - \frac{1}{2} = \frac{2}{7}$ $\quad$ $\frac{10}{11} - \frac{1}{2} = \frac{9}{22}$

PAGE 20

$\frac{1}{2}$ of a mile

$\frac{1}{4}$ of a quart

$\frac{5}{12}$ of a cup

$\frac{7}{24}$ of a pound

PAGE 21

$\frac{1}{9} + \frac{1}{3} = \frac{4}{9}$ $\quad$ $\frac{11}{12} - \frac{1}{3} = \frac{7}{12}$

$\frac{7}{8} - \frac{1}{4} = \frac{5}{8}$ $\quad$ $\frac{1}{8} + \frac{1}{16} = \frac{3}{16}$

$\frac{17}{18} - \frac{1}{6} = \frac{7}{9}$ $\quad$ $\frac{2}{3} - \frac{5}{18} = \frac{7}{18}$

$\frac{1}{2} + \frac{5}{14} = \frac{6}{7}$ $\quad$ $\frac{7}{10} + \frac{1}{4} = \frac{19}{20}$

$\frac{2}{11} + \frac{1}{9} = \frac{29}{99}$ $\quad$ $\frac{6}{7} - \frac{3}{14} = \frac{9}{14}$

$\frac{13}{15} - \frac{2}{3} = \frac{1}{5}$ $\quad$ $\frac{7}{12} - \frac{3}{8} = \frac{5}{24}$

PAGE 22

$\frac{1}{5} + \frac{1}{2}$	$\frac{3}{4} - \frac{1}{10}$
$\frac{1}{2} + \frac{1}{6}$	$\frac{5}{6} - \frac{5}{12}$
$\frac{1}{4} + \frac{2}{5}$	$\frac{4}{5} - \frac{1}{10}$
$\frac{1}{6} + \frac{1}{4}$	$\frac{13}{15} - \frac{1}{5}$
$\frac{1}{4} + \frac{1}{8}$	$\frac{5}{6} - \frac{5}{18}$
$\frac{2}{9} + \frac{1}{3}$	$\frac{7}{8} - \frac{1}{2}$

PAGE 23

START ↓

$\frac{1}{2} + \frac{2}{5}$	$\frac{7}{8} - \frac{1}{6}$	$\frac{1}{6} + \frac{1}{3}$	$\frac{1}{2} + \frac{1}{5}$	$\frac{3}{4} - \frac{1}{2}$
$\frac{8}{9} - \frac{1}{18}$	$\frac{1}{8} + \frac{3}{8}$	$\frac{3}{4} - \frac{2}{3}$	$\frac{1}{3} + \frac{5}{9}$	$\frac{2}{5} - \frac{1}{4}$
$\frac{3}{14} + \frac{1}{2}$	$\frac{9}{14} - \frac{1}{7}$	$\frac{1}{9} + \frac{1}{3}$	$\frac{1}{3} + \frac{1}{6}$	$\frac{1}{5} + \frac{2}{3}$
$\frac{1}{3} + \frac{1}{5}$	$\frac{3}{5} + \frac{2}{9}$	$\frac{3}{4} + \frac{2}{11}$	$\frac{5}{9} - \frac{1}{18}$	$\frac{5}{14} + \frac{1}{7}$
$\frac{6}{7} - \frac{1}{14}$	$\frac{3}{5} + \frac{1}{5}$	$\frac{5}{6} - \frac{1}{9}$	$\frac{1}{4} + \frac{1}{4}$	$\frac{1}{5} + \frac{4}{5}$

FINISH ↓

PAGE 24

$\frac{7}{10} - \frac{9}{20} = \frac{1}{4}$ $\quad$ $\frac{5}{24} + \frac{17}{48} = \frac{9}{16}$

$\frac{33}{64} - \frac{5}{32} = \frac{23}{64}$ $\quad$ $\frac{6}{25} + \frac{8}{75} = \frac{26}{75}$

$\frac{3}{4} - \frac{21}{40} = \frac{9}{40}$ $\quad$ $\frac{20}{27} - \frac{4}{81} = \frac{56}{81}$

$\frac{1}{2} + \frac{2}{15} = \frac{19}{30}$ $\quad$ $\frac{5}{16} + \frac{7}{12} = \frac{43}{48}$

$\frac{17}{30} - \frac{7}{15} = \frac{1}{10}$ $\quad$ $\frac{7}{100} - \frac{3}{50} = \frac{1}{100}$

$\frac{9}{16} - \frac{1}{12} = \frac{23}{48}$ $\quad$ $\frac{4}{25} - \frac{7}{75} = \frac{1}{15}$

$\frac{1}{27} + \frac{25}{54} = \frac{1}{2}$

PAGE 25

$2\frac{2}{5}$

$3\frac{1}{3}$

$1\frac{7}{8}$

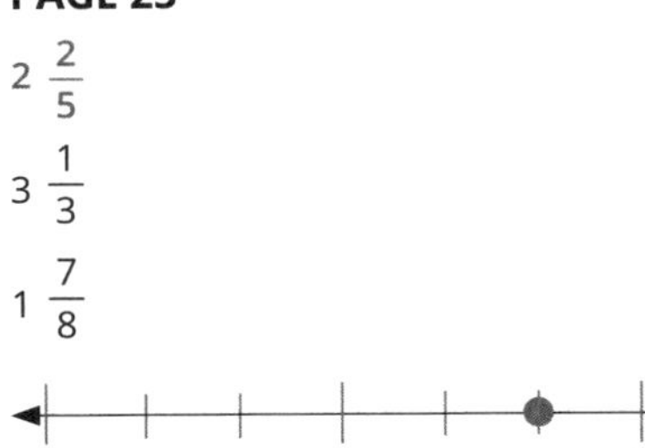

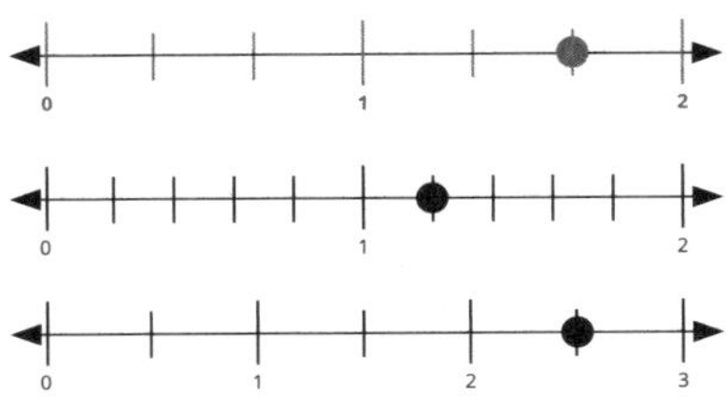

PAGE 26

$3\frac{1}{2} = \frac{7}{2}$

$2\frac{5}{6} = \frac{17}{6}$

$2\frac{1}{8} = \frac{17}{8}$

PAGE 26, *continued*

$2\frac{1}{3} = \frac{7}{3}$

$3\frac{1}{4} = \frac{13}{4}$

$1\frac{3}{5} = \frac{8}{5}$

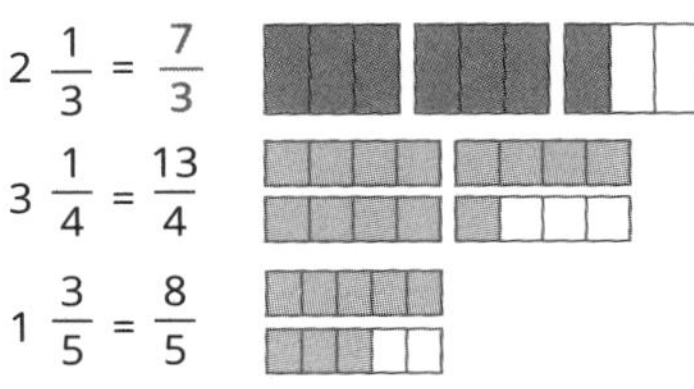

PAGE 27

$1\frac{1}{2} = \frac{3}{2}$ $\quad$ $3\frac{2}{4} = \frac{14}{4}$ $\quad$ $2\frac{1}{7} = \frac{15}{7}$

$1\frac{4}{6} = \frac{10}{6}$ $\quad$ $3\frac{3}{10} = \frac{33}{10}$ $\quad$ $3\frac{1}{6} = \frac{19}{6}$

$2\frac{2}{5} = \frac{12}{5}$ $\quad$ $3\frac{6}{7} = \frac{27}{7}$ $\quad$ $1\frac{7}{8} = \frac{15}{8}$

$2\frac{5}{9} = \frac{23}{9}$ $\quad$ $1\frac{1}{11} = \frac{12}{11}$ $\quad$ $4\frac{1}{12} = \frac{49}{12}$

Answers may vary. One possible answer is shown below.

To convert mixed numbers to improper fractions, multiply the whole number by the denominator, and then add the numerator. Write this new numerator over the original denominator.

PAGE 28

$\frac{6}{4} = 1\frac{2}{4} = 1\frac{1}{2}$ $\quad$ $\frac{11}{6} = 1\frac{5}{6}$

$\frac{9}{2} = 4\frac{1}{2}$ $\quad$ $\frac{22}{8} = 2\frac{6}{8} = 2\frac{3}{4}$

$\frac{16}{9} = 1\frac{7}{9}$ $\quad$ $\frac{18}{4} = 4\frac{2}{4} = 4\frac{1}{2}$

$\frac{34}{8} = 4\frac{2}{8} = 4\frac{1}{4}$ $\quad$ $\frac{36}{7} = 5\frac{1}{7}$

$\frac{16}{12} = 1\frac{4}{12} = 1\frac{1}{3}$ $\quad$ $\frac{31}{11} = 2\frac{9}{11}$

Answers may vary. One possible answer is shown below.

To convert improper fractions to mixed numbers, divide the numerator by the denominator. Then write the remainder as a fraction over the original denominator.

Answer key

PAGE 29

$\frac{19}{6}$ — $3\frac{1}{6}$

$\frac{11}{4}$ — $2\frac{3}{4}$

$\frac{20}{12}$ — $1\frac{2}{3}$

$\frac{22}{10}$ — $2\frac{1}{5}$

$\frac{41}{12}$ — $3\frac{5}{12}$

$\frac{18}{8}$ — $2\frac{1}{4}$

$\frac{33}{9}$ — $3\frac{2}{3}$

PAGE 30

$1\frac{1}{2} + 2\frac{1}{6} = 3\frac{2}{3}$

$\frac{2}{9} + 4\frac{1}{9} = 4\frac{1}{3}$

$1\frac{1}{6} + 6\frac{7}{12} = 7\frac{3}{4}$

$7\frac{1}{5} + 3\frac{1}{2} = 10\frac{7}{10}$

$9\frac{3}{4} + \frac{1}{8} = 9\frac{7}{8}$

$6\frac{1}{4} + 8\frac{2}{3} = 14\frac{11}{12}$

PAGE 31

$2\frac{2}{3} + 2\frac{1}{2} = 5\frac{1}{6}$

$1\frac{7}{12} + 4\frac{5}{6} = 6\frac{5}{12}$

$7\frac{5}{7} + \frac{11}{14} = 8\frac{1}{2}$

$10\frac{4}{5} + 1\frac{1}{2} = 12\frac{3}{10}$

$6\frac{3}{4} + 1\frac{7}{10} = 8\frac{9}{20}$

$9\frac{1}{3} + \frac{4}{5} = 10\frac{2}{15}$

PAGE 32

$1\frac{5}{8} + 3\frac{7}{12} = 5\frac{5}{24}$

$3\frac{1}{7} + 7\frac{1}{2} = 10\frac{9}{14}$

PAGE 32, *continued*

$5\frac{7}{9} + 2\frac{5}{9} = 8\frac{1}{3}$

$7\frac{2}{3} + 1\frac{7}{8} = 9\frac{13}{24}$

$4\frac{3}{5} + 3\frac{5}{6} = 8\frac{13}{30}$

$9\frac{3}{4} + 1\frac{4}{5} = 11\frac{11}{20}$

$2\frac{1}{3} + 3\frac{1}{3} + 2\frac{11}{12} = 8\frac{7}{12}$

$7\frac{1}{4} + 1\frac{7}{8} + 1\frac{1}{2} = 10\frac{5}{8}$

$1\frac{2}{3} + 2\frac{3}{4} + 6\frac{5}{6} = 11\frac{1}{4}$

PAGE 33

$4\frac{1}{3}$ cups of flour

$3\frac{1}{4}$ hours

$8\frac{5}{8}$ pounds of food

$8\frac{1}{8}$ laps

PAGE 34

$5\frac{1}{4} - 2\frac{1}{8} = 3\frac{1}{8}$

$9\frac{3}{4} - 4\frac{1}{4} = 5\frac{1}{2}$

$7\frac{11}{12} - 3\frac{2}{3} = 4\frac{1}{4}$

$8\frac{4}{5} - 1\frac{1}{2} = 7\frac{3}{10}$

$11\frac{1}{2} - 6\frac{1}{7} = 5\frac{5}{14}$

$9\frac{7}{10} - 8\frac{1}{5} = 1\frac{1}{2}$

PAGE 35

$4\frac{1}{4} - 1\frac{1}{2} = 2\frac{3}{4}$

$3\frac{1}{3} - 1\frac{5}{9} = 1\frac{7}{9}$

$6\frac{1}{12} - 4\frac{3}{4} = 1\frac{1}{3}$

$5\frac{1}{6} - 3\frac{3}{4} = 1\frac{5}{12}$

PAGE 35, *continued*

$11 - 4\frac{7}{8} = 6\frac{1}{8}$

$12\frac{1}{3} - \frac{5}{7} = 11\frac{13}{21}$

PAGE 36

$4\frac{1}{8} - \frac{1}{2} = 3\frac{5}{8}$

$7\frac{3}{4} - 3\frac{5}{6} = 3\frac{11}{12}$

$8\frac{1}{5} - 3\frac{6}{7} = 4\frac{12}{35}$

$5 - 2\frac{6}{7} = 2\frac{1}{7}$

$11\frac{1}{4} - 9\frac{1}{2} = 1\frac{3}{4}$

$3\frac{2}{5} - 1\frac{5}{6} = 1\frac{17}{30}$

$8\frac{3}{8} - 4\frac{5}{6} = 3\frac{13}{24}$

$5\frac{5}{18} - 2\frac{7}{9} = 2\frac{1}{2}$

$12 - 1\frac{7}{12} = 10\frac{5}{12}$

PAGE 37

$1\frac{1}{6}$ yards of rope

$1\frac{7}{8}$ pizzas

$2\frac{2}{3}$ hours

$7\frac{7}{10}$ miles

PAGE 38

$\frac{2}{5} - \frac{1}{3} = \frac{1}{15}$

$3\frac{7}{12} + 2\frac{1}{6} = 5\frac{3}{4}$

$7\frac{3}{4} - 5\frac{2}{7} = 2\frac{13}{28}$

$\frac{4}{5} + \frac{9}{10} = 1\frac{7}{10}$

$\frac{4}{11} + 7\frac{1}{2} = 7\frac{19}{22}$

$4\frac{1}{8} - 2\frac{2}{3} = 1\frac{11}{24}$

PAGE 38, *continued*

$3\frac{1}{4} + \frac{7}{9} = 4\frac{1}{36}$

$\frac{6}{7} + \frac{1}{3} = 1\frac{4}{21}$

$8 - \frac{5}{7} = 7\frac{2}{7}$

$2\frac{3}{5} + 3\frac{1}{7} = 5\frac{26}{35}$

$4 - 1\frac{11}{12} = 2\frac{1}{12}$

$\frac{5}{6} - \frac{2}{9} = \frac{11}{18}$

PAGE 39

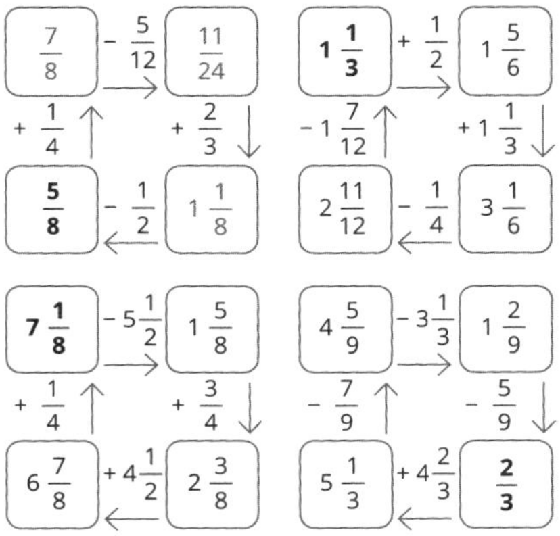

$\frac{7}{8}$	$-\frac{5}{12}$ →	$\frac{11}{24}$
$+\frac{1}{4}$ ↑		$+\frac{2}{3}$ ↓
$\frac{5}{8}$	← $-\frac{1}{2}$	$1\frac{1}{8}$

$1\frac{1}{3}$	$+\frac{1}{2}$ →	$1\frac{5}{6}$
$-1\frac{7}{12}$ ↑		$+1\frac{1}{3}$ ↓
$2\frac{11}{12}$	← $-\frac{1}{4}$	$3\frac{1}{6}$

$7\frac{1}{8}$	$-5\frac{1}{2}$ →	$1\frac{5}{8}$
$+\frac{1}{4}$ ↑		$+\frac{3}{4}$ ↓
$6\frac{7}{8}$	← $+4\frac{1}{2}$	$2\frac{3}{8}$

$4\frac{5}{9}$	$-3\frac{1}{3}$ →	$1\frac{2}{9}$
$-\frac{7}{9}$ ↑		$-\frac{5}{9}$ ↓
$5\frac{1}{3}$	← $+4\frac{2}{3}$	**$\frac{2}{3}$**

PAGE 40

$\frac{1}{2} + \frac{1}{4} > \frac{1}{3} + \frac{1}{6}$

$\frac{4}{5} + \frac{1}{2} = 2\frac{7}{10} - 1\frac{2}{5}$

$\frac{5}{8} - \frac{1}{2} < \frac{1}{4} + \frac{1}{8}$

$3\frac{3}{4} + 5\frac{1}{3} > 10 - 1\frac{7}{12}$

$\frac{11}{12} + \frac{1}{4} > 1\frac{5}{12} - \frac{2}{3}$

$\frac{1}{7} + \frac{3}{4} < \frac{5}{6} + \frac{4}{5}$

$\frac{7}{8} + \frac{3}{4} > 3 - 2\frac{1}{4}$

$8\frac{1}{6} - 4\frac{11}{12} > 5\frac{3}{10} - 2\frac{2}{5}$

$2\frac{8}{9} + 1\frac{5}{6} > 6\frac{1}{4} - 1\frac{7}{8}$

PAGE 41

($\frac{1}{8} + \frac{1}{4}$)	$\frac{1}{2} - \frac{1}{4}$	$1\frac{1}{4} - 1\frac{1}{8}$
($\frac{3}{8} + \frac{1}{6}$)	**($1\frac{1}{9} - \frac{1}{2}$)**	$2\frac{3}{4} - 2\frac{1}{3}$
($\frac{3}{4} + \frac{1}{3}$)	$3\frac{3}{5} - 2\frac{5}{7}$	$\frac{1}{5} + \frac{7}{9}$
$5 - 3\frac{3}{4}$	**($\frac{3}{4} + \frac{7}{8}$)**	**($7\frac{1}{4} - 5\frac{2}{3}$)**

PAGE 42

$p = \frac{3}{14}$ $n = 1\frac{7}{15}$

$a = 6\frac{1}{4}$ $r = \frac{1}{6}$

$y = \frac{1}{3}$ $m = 3\frac{5}{12}$

$k = \frac{1}{8}$

PAGE 43

$\frac{1}{12}$ $\frac{3}{4}$ $1\frac{1}{3}$ $3\frac{3}{5}$ $1\frac{1}{2}$

PAGE 44

Rule: add $\frac{3}{4}$	2	$2\frac{3}{4}$	$3\frac{1}{2}$	$4\frac{1}{4}$	5

Rule: subtract $\frac{3}{8}$	$9\frac{1}{4}$	$8\frac{7}{8}$	$8\frac{1}{2}$	$8\frac{1}{8}$	$7\frac{3}{4}$

Rule: add $2\frac{1}{5}$	$\frac{3}{10}$	$2\frac{1}{2}$	$4\frac{7}{10}$	$6\frac{9}{10}$	$9\frac{1}{10}$

Rule: subtract $\frac{1}{3}$	$2\frac{5}{6}$	$2\frac{1}{2}$	$2\frac{1}{6}$	$1\frac{5}{6}$	$1\frac{1}{2}$

Rule: add $\frac{1}{10}$	$\frac{7}{10}$	$\frac{4}{5}$	$\frac{9}{10}$	1	$1\frac{1}{10}$	$1\frac{1}{5}$

Rule: subtract $\frac{1}{4}$	$7\frac{3}{4}$	$7\frac{1}{2}$	$7\frac{1}{4}$	7	$6\frac{3}{4}$	$6\frac{1}{2}$

PAGE 45

$\frac{19}{24}$

$\frac{19}{30}$

$1\frac{5}{6}$ loaves

4 inches

PAGE 46

$8\frac{1}{4}$ miles

$7\frac{3}{8}$ miles

$\frac{7}{8}$ of a mile

$\frac{5}{8}$ of a mile

PAGE 47

$4 \times \frac{1}{8} = \frac{1}{2}$ $4 \times \frac{1}{5} = \frac{4}{5}$

$3 \times \frac{2}{9} = \frac{2}{3}$ $2 \times \frac{1}{4} = \frac{1}{2}$

PAGE 48

$4 \times \frac{1}{10} = \frac{2}{5}$ $10 \times \frac{1}{7} = 1\frac{3}{7}$

$\frac{1}{3} \times 8 = 2\frac{2}{3}$ $1 \times \frac{4}{9} = \frac{4}{9}$

$\frac{4}{5} \times 6 = 4\frac{4}{5}$ $\frac{3}{4} \times 3 = 2\frac{1}{4}$

$2 \times \frac{1}{8} = \frac{1}{4}$ $11 \times \frac{4}{11} = 4$

$7 \times \frac{3}{5} = 4\frac{1}{5}$ $\frac{5}{8} \times 4 = 2\frac{1}{2}$

PAGE 49

$\frac{2}{3} \times 7 = 4\frac{2}{3}$ $6 \times \frac{1}{2} = 3$

$11 \times \frac{3}{4} = 8\frac{1}{4}$ $\frac{5}{6} \times 4 = 3\frac{1}{3}$

$7 \times \frac{1}{5} = 1\frac{2}{5}$ $2 \times \frac{4}{9} = \frac{8}{9}$

$5 \times \frac{1}{3} = 1\frac{2}{3}$ $8 \times \frac{3}{8} = 3$

$\frac{2}{3} \times 3 = 2$ $\frac{5}{12} \times 7 = 2\frac{11}{12}$

$\frac{3}{5} \times 15 = 9$ $16 \times \frac{2}{9} = 3\frac{5}{9}$

$20 \times \frac{4}{7} = 11\frac{3}{7}$ $\frac{2}{3} \times 17 = 11\frac{1}{3}$

Answer key

PAGE 50

$\frac{5}{11} \times 9 = \frac{45}{11}$ or $4\frac{1}{11}$

$\frac{3}{4} \times 7 = \frac{21}{4}$ or $5\frac{1}{4}$

$5 \times \frac{5}{6} = \frac{25}{6}$ or $4\frac{1}{6}$

$2 \times \frac{3}{8} = \frac{6}{8}$ or $\frac{3}{4}$

$\frac{2}{9} \times 8 = \frac{16}{9}$ or $1\frac{7}{9}$

$\frac{3}{4} \times 4 = \frac{12}{4}$ or 3

$8 \times \frac{6}{7} = \frac{48}{7}$ or $6\frac{6}{7}$

$6 \times \frac{4}{5} = \frac{24}{5}$ or $4\frac{4}{5}$

$7 \times \frac{3}{10} = \frac{21}{10}$ or $2\frac{1}{10}$

$\frac{4}{11} \times 9 = \frac{36}{11}$ or $3\frac{3}{11}$

PAGE 51

$\frac{2}{3}$ of 12 = 8

$\frac{1}{2}$ of 14 = 7

$\frac{1}{5}$ of 11 = $2\frac{1}{5}$

$\frac{3}{4}$ of 4 = 3

$\frac{1}{6}$ of 11 = $1\frac{5}{6}$

$\frac{1}{4}$ of 3 = $\frac{3}{4}$

$\frac{5}{7}$ of 9 = $6\frac{3}{7}$

$\frac{2}{3}$ of 10 = $6\frac{2}{3}$

$\frac{1}{8}$ of 7 = $\frac{7}{8}$

PAGE 52

6 friends
10 miles
3 racing games
4 friends

PAGE 53

$1\frac{1}{2}$ onions

$2\frac{2}{3}$ cups

$\frac{3}{4}$ tsp.

$4\frac{1}{4}$ tsp.

PAGE 54

$\frac{2}{3} \times \frac{1}{2} = \frac{1}{3}$

$\frac{1}{4} \times \frac{3}{4} = \frac{3}{16}$

$\frac{1}{3} \times \frac{4}{9} = \frac{4}{27}$

$\frac{1}{8} \times \frac{5}{6} = \frac{5}{48}$

$\frac{7}{10} \times \frac{3}{8} = \frac{21}{80}$

$\frac{7}{12} \times \frac{1}{2} = \frac{7}{24}$

$\frac{7}{8} \times \frac{2}{3} = \frac{7}{12}$

$\frac{1}{12} \times \frac{1}{4} = \frac{1}{48}$

$\frac{1}{6} \times \frac{3}{4} = \frac{1}{8}$

$\frac{3}{11} \times \frac{1}{3} = \frac{1}{11}$

$\frac{7}{10} \times \frac{4}{5} = \frac{14}{25}$

PAGE 55

$\frac{2}{5} \times \frac{1}{3} = \frac{2}{15}$

$\frac{3}{10} \times \frac{1}{2} = \frac{3}{20}$

$\frac{5}{6} \times \frac{2}{7} = \frac{5}{21}$

$\frac{5}{8} \times \frac{1}{3} = \frac{5}{24}$

$\frac{8}{9} \times \frac{2}{9} = \frac{16}{81}$

$\frac{1}{5} \times \frac{3}{4} = \frac{3}{20}$

$\frac{9}{10} \times \frac{3}{4} = \frac{27}{40}$

$\frac{2}{11} \times \frac{1}{5} = \frac{2}{55}$

$\frac{5}{7} \times \frac{1}{8} = \frac{5}{56}$

$\frac{3}{5} \times \frac{1}{4} = \frac{3}{20}$

$\frac{4}{5} \times \frac{5}{12} = \frac{1}{3}$

$\frac{9}{10} \times \frac{1}{2} = \frac{9}{20}$

PAGE 56

$\frac{1}{3}$ of $\frac{4}{5} = \frac{4}{15}$

$\frac{3}{5}$ of $\frac{3}{7} = \frac{9}{35}$

$\frac{2}{7}$ of $\frac{1}{4} = \frac{1}{14}$

$\frac{5}{12}$ of $\frac{2}{3} = \frac{5}{18}$

$\frac{2}{3}$ of $\frac{1}{4} = \frac{1}{6}$

$\frac{5}{9}$ of $\frac{5}{6} = \frac{25}{54}$

$\frac{1}{2}$ of $\frac{1}{10} = \frac{1}{20}$

$\frac{2}{9}$ of $\frac{4}{7} = \frac{8}{63}$

PAGE 57

$\frac{1}{2}$

$\frac{1}{16}$

$\frac{5}{18}$

$\frac{5}{8}$

PAGE 58

$\frac{1}{8}$

$\frac{3}{8}$

$\frac{1}{4}$

Oliver

PAGE 59

$2\frac{3}{4} \times \frac{2}{5} = 1\frac{1}{10}$

$1\frac{3}{8} \times \frac{2}{3} = \frac{11}{12}$

$\frac{1}{5} \times 1\frac{3}{4} = \frac{7}{20}$

$3\frac{2}{3} \times \frac{1}{2} = 1\frac{5}{6}$

$\frac{1}{5} \times 1\frac{1}{3} = \frac{4}{15}$

$2\frac{2}{5} \times \frac{3}{5} = 1\frac{11}{25}$

$5\frac{1}{2} \times \frac{5}{12} = 2\frac{7}{24}$

PAGE 60

$2\frac{1}{2} \times 1\frac{3}{4} = 4\frac{3}{8}$

$2\frac{1}{5} \times 1\frac{1}{6} = 2\frac{17}{30}$

$1\frac{1}{9} \times 1\frac{3}{7} = 1\frac{37}{63}$

$2\frac{1}{4} \times 4\frac{1}{2} = 10\frac{1}{8}$

$1\frac{1}{11} \times 3\frac{1}{2} = 3\frac{9}{11}$

$1\frac{2}{7} \times 1\frac{2}{5} = 1\frac{4}{5}$

$5\frac{1}{4} \times 1\frac{1}{8} = 5\frac{29}{32}$

PAGE 61

$1\frac{1}{8} \times 1\frac{3}{4} < 1\frac{2}{5} \times 1\frac{2}{3}$

$4\frac{1}{2} \times \frac{1}{12} < 3\frac{2}{3} \times \frac{1}{8}$

$1\frac{1}{4} \times \frac{2}{3} > 2\frac{1}{3} \times \frac{1}{7}$

$1\frac{3}{4} \times \frac{2}{3} = 3\frac{1}{2} \times \frac{1}{3}$

$3\frac{1}{2} \times 1\frac{4}{5} > 2\frac{1}{8} \times 2\frac{2}{3}$

$2\frac{1}{10} \times 2\frac{3}{5} < 2\frac{1}{2} \times 2\frac{6}{7}$

$3\frac{2}{3} \times 4 > 3\frac{2}{5} \times 3\frac{3}{4}$

PAGE 62

$\frac{5}{8} \times 6 = 3\frac{3}{4}$

$\frac{2}{9} \times 4 = \frac{8}{9}$

$\frac{2}{7} \times \frac{1}{3} = \frac{2}{21}$

$\frac{7}{12} \times \frac{5}{6} = \frac{35}{72}$

$3\frac{6}{7} \times \frac{3}{10} = 1\frac{11}{70}$

$\frac{9}{11} \times 1\frac{2}{3} = 1\frac{4}{11}$

$9 \times 1\frac{3}{10} = 11\frac{7}{10}$

$1\frac{1}{4} \times 8 = 10$

$3\frac{4}{7} \times 1\frac{8}{9} = 6\frac{47}{63}$

$2\frac{1}{8} \times 2\frac{2}{3} = 5\frac{2}{3}$

PAGE 63

$6\frac{2}{3}$ cups

$1\frac{9}{16}$ miles

$7\frac{1}{2}$ hours

$11\frac{1}{4}$ acres

$1\frac{1}{4}$ cups

PAGE 64

$3 \times 1\frac{1}{2} = 4\frac{1}{2}$ The product is greater than 3.

$3 \times \frac{3}{5} = 1\frac{4}{5}$ The product is less than 3.

$3 \times 1 = 3$ The product is equal to 3.

When the second number is larger than 1, the product will be greater than 3. When the second number is less than 1, the product will be less than 3. When the second number is 1, the product will be equal to 3.

PAGE 64, *continued*

$8 \times \frac{1}{2}$ will be less than 8.

$\frac{1}{3} \times 3\frac{3}{4}$ will be greater than $\frac{1}{3}$.

$2 \times 1\frac{5}{12}$ will be greater than 2.

$\frac{7}{8} \times \frac{8}{9}$ will be less than $\frac{7}{8}$.

PAGE 65

$12 \times \frac{1}{9} < 12 \times 1\frac{1}{9}$

$\frac{8}{15} \times 2\frac{1}{5} > \frac{8}{15} \times \frac{1}{5}$

$156 \times 4\frac{1}{7} > 156 \times \frac{4}{7}$

$8 \times \frac{6}{7} < 8 \times 1\frac{1}{8}$

$22 \times \frac{1}{6} < 32 \times \frac{1}{6}$

$94 \times 1\frac{1}{4} > 90 \times \frac{2}{3}$

$16 \times 1\frac{1}{8} > 15 \times \frac{7}{8}$

PAGE 66

Rule					
Rule: multiply by $\frac{1}{4}$	$\frac{1}{2}$	$\frac{1}{8}$	$\frac{1}{32}$	$\frac{1}{128}$	$\frac{1}{512}$
Rule: multiply by 2	$\frac{2}{3}$	$1\frac{1}{3}$	$2\frac{2}{3}$	$5\frac{1}{3}$	$10\frac{2}{3}$
Rule: multiply by $\frac{1}{2}$	$\frac{2}{5}$	$\frac{1}{5}$	$\frac{1}{10}$	$\frac{1}{20}$	$\frac{1}{40}$
Rule: multiply by $1\frac{1}{3}$	$\frac{1}{6}$	$\frac{2}{9}$	$\frac{8}{27}$	$\frac{32}{81}$	$\frac{128}{243}$
Rule: multiply by 4	$\frac{1}{12}$	$\frac{1}{3}$	$1\frac{1}{3}$	$5\frac{1}{3}$	$21\frac{1}{3}$
Rule: multiply by $2\frac{1}{2}$	$\frac{1}{3}$	$\frac{5}{6}$	$2\frac{1}{12}$	$5\frac{5}{24}$	$13\frac{1}{48}$

PAGE 67

$4 \div \frac{1}{2} = 8$

$2 \div \frac{1}{4} = 8$

$4 \div \frac{1}{3} = 12$

$2 \div \frac{1}{6} = 12$

PAGE 68

Placement of shading may vary.

$\frac{1}{2} \div 4 = \frac{1}{8}$

$\frac{1}{5} \div 3 = \frac{1}{15}$

$\frac{1}{3} \div 4 = \frac{1}{12}$

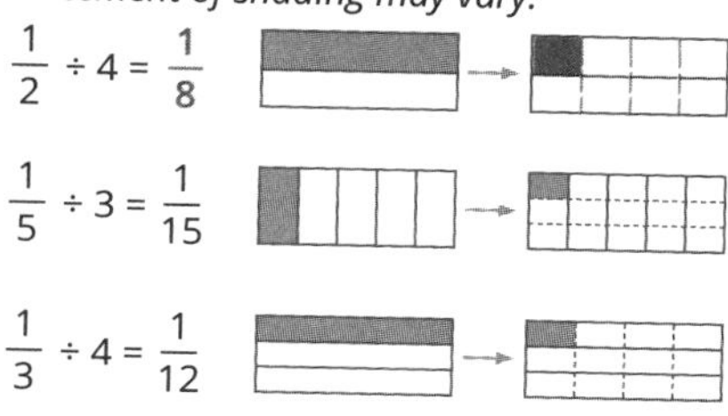

$\frac{1}{4} \div 2 = \frac{1}{8}$

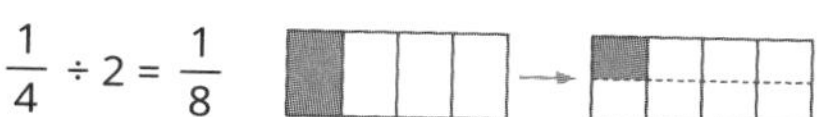

PAGE 69

Drawings and shading may vary.

$\frac{1}{2} \div 3 = \frac{1}{6}$ $2 \div \frac{1}{3} = 6$

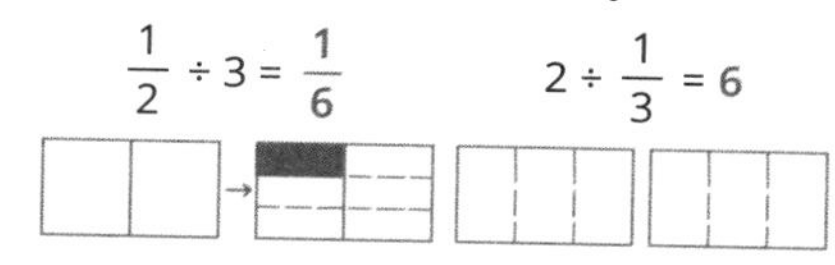

$\frac{1}{5} \div 2 = \frac{1}{10}$ $5 \div \frac{1}{2} = 10$

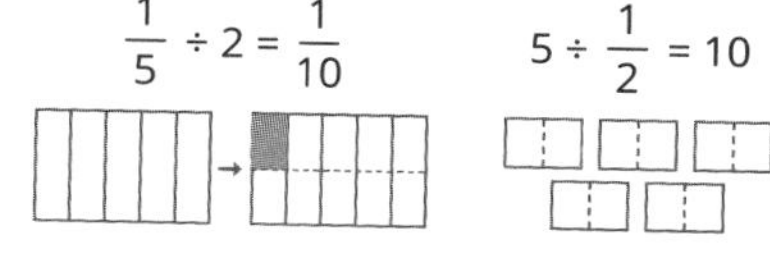

$\frac{1}{3} \div 5 = \frac{1}{15}$ $3 \div \frac{1}{5} = 15$

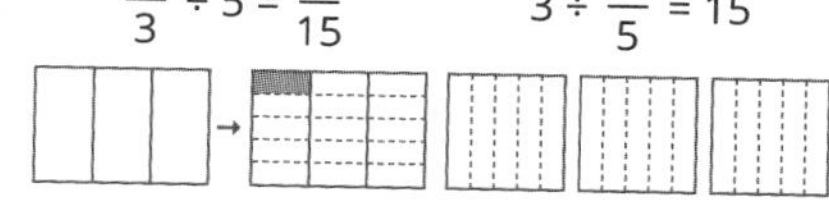

$\frac{1}{4} \div 3 = \frac{1}{12}$ $4 \div \frac{1}{3} = 12$

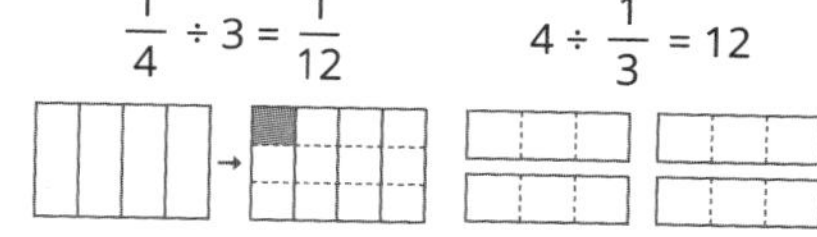

Answers may vary. One possible answer is shown below.

For each pair of problems, the whole numbers and the denominators switch places. You can see the same number in each pair's answers, either as a whole number or as the denominator of a fraction.

Answer key

PAGE 70

$\frac{2}{7} \rightarrow \frac{7}{2}$

$\frac{1}{2} \rightarrow \frac{2}{1}$ or 2

$5 \rightarrow \frac{1}{5}$

$\frac{9}{11} \rightarrow \frac{11}{9}$

$\frac{5}{6} \rightarrow \frac{6}{5}$

$\frac{4}{5} \rightarrow \frac{5}{4}$

$\frac{6}{7} \rightarrow \frac{7}{6}$

$8 \rightarrow \frac{1}{8}$

$\frac{2}{9} \rightarrow \frac{9}{2}$

$\frac{7}{12} \rightarrow \frac{12}{7}$

$2 \rightarrow \frac{1}{2}$

PAGE 71

$\frac{5}{7} \div 3 = \frac{5}{21}$

$7 \div \frac{2}{3} = 10\frac{1}{2}$

$\frac{4}{5} \div 3 = \frac{4}{15}$

$9 \div \frac{7}{10} = 12\frac{6}{7}$

$\frac{1}{2} \div 2 = \frac{1}{4}$

$\frac{2}{5} \div 4 = \frac{1}{10}$

$\frac{1}{4} \div 8 = \frac{1}{32}$

$11 \div \frac{3}{5} = 18\frac{1}{3}$

PAGE 72

$\frac{1}{3} \div \frac{2}{9} = 1\frac{1}{2}$

$\frac{2}{3} \div \frac{8}{9} = \frac{3}{4}$

$\frac{1}{3} \div \frac{9}{11} = \frac{11}{27}$

$\frac{5}{7} \div \frac{3}{4} = \frac{20}{21}$

$\frac{5}{6} \div \frac{2}{9} = 3\frac{3}{4}$

$\frac{1}{9} \div \frac{1}{4} = \frac{4}{9}$

$\frac{1}{9} \div \frac{4}{5} = \frac{5}{36}$

$\frac{3}{5} \div \frac{1}{4} = 2\frac{2}{5}$

$\frac{10}{11} \div \frac{1}{5} = 4\frac{6}{11}$

$\frac{1}{3} \div \frac{5}{12} = \frac{4}{5}$

PAGE 73

$\frac{2}{5} \div \frac{3}{11} = 1\frac{7}{15}$

$\frac{9}{10} \div \frac{1}{2} = 1\frac{4}{5}$

$\frac{2}{9} \div \frac{5}{9} = \frac{2}{5}$

$\frac{1}{5} \div \frac{4}{9} = \frac{9}{20}$

$\frac{1}{6} \div \frac{1}{9} = 1\frac{1}{2}$

$\frac{9}{10} \div \frac{1}{10} = 9$

$\frac{1}{8} \div \frac{3}{5} = \frac{5}{24}$

$\frac{5}{12} \div \frac{1}{7} = 2\frac{11}{12}$

$\frac{3}{7} \div \frac{2}{3} = \frac{9}{14}$

$\frac{7}{11} \div \frac{2}{3} = \frac{21}{22}$

$\frac{6}{7} \div \frac{1}{6} = 5\frac{1}{7}$

$\frac{7}{12} \div \frac{1}{6} = 3\frac{1}{2}$

PAGE 74

$2 \div \frac{3}{4}$	21
$\frac{5}{7} \div \frac{1}{9}$	$3\frac{1}{5}$
$\frac{1}{2} \div \frac{4}{7}$	$2\frac{2}{3}$
$\frac{9}{10} \div 4$	$\frac{7}{8}$
$3 \div \frac{1}{7}$	$6\frac{3}{7}$
$\frac{4}{5} \div \frac{1}{4}$	$\frac{9}{40}$

PAGE 75

$6 \div \frac{2}{3} > 4 \div \frac{1}{2}$

$\frac{1}{6} \div \frac{4}{5} = \frac{1}{8} \div \frac{3}{5}$

$\frac{1}{12} \div \frac{1}{8} < \frac{5}{6} \div \frac{2}{3}$

$\frac{5}{6} \div \frac{1}{9} > \frac{3}{4} \div \frac{1}{7}$

$10 \div \frac{2}{3} = 5 \div \frac{1}{3}$

$\frac{3}{11} \div \frac{1}{2} < \frac{7}{11} \div \frac{1}{6}$

PAGE 76

$\frac{1}{16}$ of a gallon

$\frac{2}{7}$

56 servings

6 more days

PAGE 77

$10 \div 7 = 1\frac{3}{7}$

$15 \div 25 = \frac{3}{5}$

$35 \div 20 = 1\frac{3}{4}$

$5 \div 60 = \frac{1}{12}$

$16 \div 36 = \frac{4}{9}$

$9 \div 75 = \frac{3}{25}$

$8 \div 18 = \frac{4}{9}$

$24 \div 10 = 2\frac{2}{5}$

$36 \div 42 = \frac{6}{7}$

$48 \div 22 = 2\frac{2}{11}$

$72 \div 11 = 6\frac{6}{11}$

$80 \div 15 = 5\frac{1}{3}$

PAGE 78

$1\frac{1}{3}$ quarts

$\frac{3}{4}$ of an ounce

$\frac{1}{6}$ of a pound

$3\frac{3}{4}$ cups

$8\frac{1}{2}$ minutes

PAGE 79

$\frac{5}{6} + \frac{1}{4} = 1\frac{1}{12}$

$7 - 1\frac{3}{4} = 5\frac{1}{4}$

$9 \times \frac{5}{6} = 7\frac{1}{2}$

$2\frac{7}{9} + 1\frac{2}{3} = 4\frac{4}{9}$

$\frac{5}{8} - \frac{1}{7} = \frac{27}{56}$

$\frac{1}{2} \times \frac{5}{7} = \frac{5}{14}$

$4 \div \frac{2}{5} = 10$

$4\frac{1}{3} + \frac{1}{9} = 4\frac{4}{9}$

$\frac{3}{4} \div \frac{2}{3} = 1\frac{1}{8}$

$12 \times \frac{8}{9} = 10\frac{2}{3}$

$\frac{1}{9} \div \frac{5}{6} = \frac{2}{15}$

$10\frac{5}{12} - 5\frac{1}{6} = 5\frac{1}{4}$

PAGE 80

START				FINISH
$\frac{1}{2}$	$\times \frac{1}{2}$ →	$\frac{1}{4}$		$6\frac{13}{15}$
		↓ $+\frac{3}{8}$		↑ $-\frac{1}{6}$
$1\frac{1}{8}$	$+\frac{1}{2}$ ←	$\frac{5}{8}$		$7\frac{1}{30}$
↓ $\times 4$				↑ $+4\frac{1}{3}$
$4\frac{1}{2}$	$-3\frac{3}{5}$ →	$\frac{9}{10}$	$\div \frac{1}{3}$ →	$2\frac{7}{10}$

PAGE 81

$\frac{1}{2} \times \frac{5}{3} = \frac{5}{6}$

$\frac{5}{6} - \frac{2}{3} = \frac{1}{6}$

$6 \div \frac{1}{4} = 24$

$\frac{1}{3} + \frac{1}{2} = \frac{5}{6}$

$1\frac{3}{4} \times \frac{1}{8} = \frac{7}{32}$

$\frac{1}{5} + \frac{3}{10} = \frac{1}{2}$

$\frac{7}{10} + \frac{2}{5} = 1\frac{1}{10}$

$1\frac{1}{8} - \frac{3}{4} = \frac{3}{8}$

$\frac{2}{5} \times \frac{5}{6} = \frac{1}{3}$

$\frac{1}{7} \div \frac{1}{2} = \frac{2}{7}$

PAGE 82

8 $\quad \frac{1}{8} \quad \frac{2}{3} \quad 1\frac{1}{7} \quad 4\frac{1}{11} \quad 5\frac{8}{15}$

PAGE 83

4 friends

$2\frac{1}{2}$ teaspoons

$12\frac{3}{8}$ pounds

$1\frac{1}{6}$ pounds

PAGE 84

$2\frac{5}{6}$ cups

$1\frac{1}{3}$ cups

$2\frac{1}{2}$ cups

$\frac{3}{8}$ of a cup

PAGE 85

11 ft.

$\frac{3}{8}$ in.

$16\frac{1}{4}$ ft.

5 in.

$20\frac{1}{5}$ m

PAGE 86

$4\frac{2}{3}$ in.

$3\frac{1}{2}$ m

$\frac{3}{4}$ in.

$2\frac{3}{4}$ in.

PAGE 87

$2\frac{1}{4}$ ft.^{2}

$\frac{1}{4}$ in.^{2}

$7\frac{1}{5}$ cm^2

$\frac{1}{25}$ m^2

$5\frac{1}{16}$ ft.^{2}

$3\frac{15}{16}$ in.^{2}

PAGE 88

12 ft.^{2}

$\frac{3}{32}$ ft.^{2}

$\frac{3}{5}$ m^2

PAGE 89

$18\frac{7}{9}$ square feet

$\frac{21}{25}$ of a square meter

The window in Brandon's kitchen is $12\frac{3}{8}$ square feet. So, the window in his bedroom is $\frac{1}{4}$ of a square foot larger.

$\frac{4}{5}$ of a meter

PAGE 90

$\frac{1}{3} + \frac{1}{3} = \frac{2}{3}$

$\frac{11}{12} - \frac{3}{4} = \frac{1}{6}$

$\frac{3}{5} + \frac{1}{9} = \frac{32}{45}$

$\frac{3}{4} + \frac{2}{5} = 1\frac{3}{20}$

$\frac{9}{10} - \frac{1}{3} = \frac{17}{30}$

$\frac{4}{7} + \frac{1}{2} = 1\frac{1}{14}$

$\frac{3}{7} + \frac{2}{7} = \frac{5}{7}$

$\frac{2}{3} - \frac{1}{6} = \frac{1}{2}$

$\frac{7}{9} - \frac{1}{4} = \frac{19}{36}$

$\frac{5}{6} + \frac{1}{2} = 1\frac{1}{3}$

$\frac{8}{11} - \frac{1}{4} = \frac{21}{44}$

$\frac{7}{12} - \frac{3}{8} = \frac{5}{24}$

PAGE 91

$2\frac{1}{2} + \frac{1}{3} = 2\frac{5}{6}$

$4\frac{5}{6} - 2\frac{1}{3} = 2\frac{1}{2}$

$5\frac{1}{7} - \frac{3}{4} = 4\frac{11}{28}$

$6\frac{1}{2} + 4\frac{4}{5} = 11\frac{3}{10}$

$2\frac{1}{2} - 1\frac{1}{8} = 1\frac{3}{8}$

$7 + 4\frac{1}{12} = 11\frac{1}{12}$

$4 - 2\frac{7}{9} = 1\frac{2}{9}$

$6\frac{2}{3} - \frac{1}{2} = 6\frac{1}{6}$

$1\frac{3}{8} + \frac{1}{5} = 1\frac{23}{40}$

$7\frac{1}{10} - \frac{4}{5} = 6\frac{3}{10}$

$9\frac{1}{4} - \frac{6}{7} = 8\frac{11}{28}$

$1\frac{2}{3} + 4\frac{4}{5} = 6\frac{7}{15}$

PAGE 92

$2\frac{2}{3}$	$\frac{1}{3}$	2
1	$1\frac{2}{3}$	$2\frac{1}{3}$
$1\frac{1}{3}$	3	$\frac{2}{3}$

$\frac{2}{3}$	$\frac{1}{2}$	$1\frac{1}{3}$
$1\frac{1}{2}$	$\frac{5}{6}$	$\frac{1}{6}$
$\frac{1}{3}$	$1\frac{1}{6}$	1

$\frac{2}{3}$	$\frac{1}{12}$	$\frac{1}{2}$
$\frac{1}{4}$	$\frac{5}{12}$	$\frac{7}{12}$
$\frac{1}{3}$	$\frac{3}{4}$	$\frac{1}{6}$

$1\frac{3}{5}$	$1\frac{7}{10}$	$1\frac{1}{5}$
$1\frac{1}{10}$	$1\frac{1}{2}$	$1\frac{9}{10}$
$1\frac{4}{5}$	$1\frac{3}{10}$	$1\frac{2}{5}$

PAGE 93

$\frac{5}{8}$

$\frac{5}{6}$

$1\frac{3}{8}$ pounds

$3\frac{5}{8}$ quarts

Answer key

PAGE 94

$5\frac{3}{5}$ m

$4\frac{4}{5}$ ft.

7 m

$16\frac{3}{4}$ in.

$3\frac{5}{8}$ in.

$2\frac{1}{8}$ in.

PAGE 95

$\frac{5}{6} \times 2 = 1\frac{2}{3}$

$\frac{4}{5} \times 9 = 7\frac{1}{5}$

$3 \times \frac{8}{9} = 2\frac{2}{3}$

$12 \times \frac{5}{12} = 5$

$\frac{1}{2} \times \frac{1}{3} = \frac{1}{6}$

$\frac{3}{4} \times \frac{2}{7} = \frac{3}{14}$

$\frac{1}{5} \times \frac{3}{8} = \frac{3}{40}$

$\frac{1}{7} \times \frac{3}{10} = \frac{3}{70}$

$\frac{5}{12} \times \frac{1}{6} = \frac{5}{72}$

$\frac{9}{11} \times \frac{1}{2} = \frac{9}{22}$

$\frac{6}{7} \times \frac{1}{9} = \frac{2}{21}$

PAGE 96

$\frac{7}{8} \times 2\frac{1}{2} = 2\frac{3}{16}$

$1\frac{3}{7} \times \frac{2}{3} = \frac{20}{21}$

$3 \times 1\frac{3}{8} = 4\frac{1}{8}$

$1\frac{1}{3} \times 3\frac{2}{3} = 4\frac{8}{9}$

$2\frac{1}{2} \times 1\frac{1}{6} = 2\frac{11}{12}$

$1\frac{1}{10} \times 2\frac{1}{4} = 2\frac{19}{40}$

$1\frac{1}{9} \times 1\frac{4}{7} = 1\frac{47}{63}$

$2\frac{3}{5} \times 2\frac{3}{4} = 7\frac{3}{20}$

$1\frac{1}{7} \times 4\frac{5}{6} = 5\frac{11}{21}$

$5\frac{8}{9} \times 1\frac{1}{4} = 7\frac{13}{36}$

PAGE 97

$1\frac{1}{16}$ in.^{2}

$12\frac{1}{4}$ in.^{2}

$2\frac{5}{8}$ in.^{2}

$\frac{9}{25}$ m^2

14 in.^{2}

6 m^2

PAGE 98

$4 \div \frac{2}{3} = 6$

$\frac{5}{6} \div 3 = \frac{5}{18}$

$\frac{3}{4} \div \frac{1}{4} = 3$

$1 \div \frac{1}{5} = 5$

$\frac{1}{2} \div 6 = \frac{1}{12}$

$\frac{1}{3} \div \frac{4}{9} = \frac{3}{4}$

$12 \div \frac{3}{4} = 16$

$\frac{3}{8} \div 12 = \frac{1}{32}$

$\frac{2}{3} \div \frac{3}{5} = 1\frac{1}{9}$

$5 \div \frac{5}{7} = 7$

$\frac{7}{9} \div 8 = \frac{7}{72}$

$\frac{7}{10} \div \frac{1}{5} = 3\frac{1}{2}$

PAGE 99

$\frac{1}{2}$ in.

$\frac{1}{4}$ ft.

$\frac{1}{4}$ in.

$\frac{3}{10}$ m

PAGE 100

$\frac{25}{64}$ ft.^{2}

$2\frac{17}{24}$ in.^{2}

$35\frac{9}{25}$ m^2

PAGE 101

$17\frac{1}{2}$ minutes

4 servings

6 flower pots

No. Camille will need 15 bunches of roses to make 4 flower arrangements.

PAGE 102

$1\frac{5}{12}$ cups

$2\frac{5}{12}$ cups

$\frac{3}{4}$ of a cup

$1\frac{1}{2}$ cups